HEALING
DREAMS

HEALING
DREAMS

How to Interpret Your Dreams
and Change Your Life

SARAH DENING

hamlyn

First published in Great Britain in 2004
by Hamlyn, a division of Octopus Publishing Group Ltd
2–4 Heron Quays, London E14 4JP

Distributed in the United States and Canada by
Sterling Publishing Co., Inc.
387 Park Avenue South, New York, NY 10016-8810

ISBN 0 600 60897 2

1 2 3 4 5 6 7 8 9 10

A CIP catalogue record for this book is available from
the British Library

Printed and bound in China

Contents

Introduction

Why are dreams healing?

The idea that dreams can be healing is not new. In the ancient civilizations of Egypt and Greece, patients who failed to respond to medical treatment could arrange to sleep in a temple especially dedicated to the god of healing. They hoped he would visit them in a dream, enabling them to regain their health. The temples of the Greek God Asclepius were especially renowned for their high success rate – and often grew rich on the contributions of grateful patients.

Native American Indians believed that dreams were sent by the Great Spirit, to act as a guiding light for your soul and prevent it from becoming lost in the darkness of ignorance. Losing touch with them would be disastrous, as you would then be unaware of your true path in life and become depressed or ill.

The eminent psychologist Carl Jung also believed in the healing power of dreams, many years of clinical experience convincing him that most of our problems are the result of losing contact with our deepest instincts. He observed that there is a way of gaining access to the age-old wisdom hidden in each of us deep within the unconscious mind. That way is through our dreams.

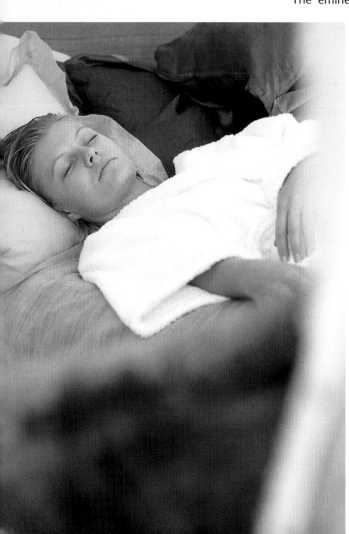

Nowadays, doctors are well aware of the link between our state of mind and physical symptoms. Stress is a major factor in ill-health, whilst suppressed feelings like rage or resentment can also disturb the body's equilibrium and create dis-ease. Our dreams are nature's way of helping us to maintain a balanced outlook. They usually contain helpful messages about the emotional adjustments we need to make from day to day. If we take these seriously, we avoid nurturing unrealistic attitudes and prevent the build-up of stress or toxic emotions.

Sometimes you may develop an illness if you secretly feel unable to face up to something and have a need for someone to take care of you. Your dreams can reveal your hidden agenda and suggest a way forward. In helping you to focus on the underlying cause of your symptoms, they enable you to participate in your own healing process.

Your dreams can further your emotional well-being by helping you to understand how your feelings and attitudes affect other people, often at a subliminal level, and can therefore create or destroy relationships. If someone has let you down, for instance, your dreams may reveal that, subconsciously, you expect people to disappoint you – and, sooner or later, that is exactly what they do. Once you wake up to the fact that relationships don't have to turn out this way, you can transform your life.

Whether you need more confidence, to have better relationships, or the courage to make the correct decisions, your dreams can guide you through even the most difficult situations and help you to become the person nature always meant you to be. I hope this book will inspire you to find out more about one of your most precious, yet most neglected natural resources – your dreams.

How to remember your dreams

Many people are convinced that they do not dream. 'My head hits the pillow and I'm out for the count', they often say, 'and when I wake up in the morning, I cannot recall having had any dreams'. Scientific research, however, confirms that we all dream at regular intervals throughout the night.

Every 90 minutes or so your eyes move rapidly around under your closed eyelids. At the same time your brainwaves become highly active, almost as though you were awake. It's during this period of what is known as 'Rapid Eye Movement' or 'REM sleep' that you dream. In the early part of the night, which is when sleep is deepest, the REM periods are quite short, lasting only a few minutes at most. Towards morning, as your sleep becomes lighter, the REM episodes become longer. The last dream you have just before waking up can last for as long as three-quarters of an hour.

During REM sleep, your body is immobilized. This means that if you have a nightmare where you try to run away or cry out, you feel paralyzed. People who walk and talk in their sleep usually do so between periods of REM sleep when the body is once again able to move.

Although some people have a natural facility for remembering their dreams, particularly those with emotional, creative or introverted personalities, few can bring back the whole experience whilst others recall little or nothing. Accurate dream recall is not easy. You learn it, as you learn any skill, by developing an interest, maintaining your enthusiasm and following a routine.

If you have a stressful lifestyle, try not to watch television late in the evening. Instead, spend a few minutes relaxing quietly and letting go of the day's concerns. If you find it hard to switch off, light reading can be helpful and alcohol and coffee late at night should be avoided. They are known to inhibit dream recall, as can sleeping pills. Keep a pen and a notebook within easy reach of your bed. Leave this special notebook open and write down the date as a signal to your subconscious mind that you intend to remember a dream.

As you start drifting off into sleep, tell yourself: 'Tonight I shall have a dream and remember it in the morning.' When you wake up, lie still and keep your eyes closed. Allow your mind to stay relaxed, drifting back until you recapture a fragment of a dream. Even a single image is better than nothing. As soon as you remember anything, write it down, however trivial it seems. Make it a habit to write something – even a note of the mood you woke up in is better than nothing. It's important to do this first thing, before you get out of bed. The simple act of changing your position in bed can be enough to make a dream disappear without trace. A loud alarm clock can have a similar effect. Do remember that no skill is acquired overnight. Be patient and persevere.

Bringing your dreams alive

Dreams speak to us in symbolic language, often using events in our everyday life, past and present, to get across their message. Since no two people are exactly alike, no two dreams have exactly the same meaning. As you will see, even the most ordinary symbol can have several different meanings.

In each case the most common interpretations are offered. But what can you do if none of them seem relevant – or if your dream features a symbol that hasn't been discussed?

Oddly enough, it would almost be better for you *not* to find an exact explanation! An interpretation that somebody else has given you, however accurate it is, will not necessarily mobilize the full healing potential of the dream. Since dreams belong to the realm of the imagination, it's through your own creative work with them that you will bring them alive and benefit most from their transformative effect.

People often tell me they're 'not creative' or 'can't use their imagination'. I always then ask them to imagine taking a bite out of a lemon. Whether you see, feel or taste it, you have used your imagination to create something that wasn't there a moment ago. It's as simple as that.

Two essential processes will help you to use your imagination to shed light on almost any dream. They are ASSOCIATION and AMPLIFICATION.

Association

This process involves all the thoughts and feelings you have about the images in your dream, together with its setting. Suppose, for instance, that you dream about a cat. Make a note of anything and everything you associate with cats. Do you like them or hate them? Does the cat in the dream resemble a pet you have, or used to have? Do cats remind you of a certain period or event in your life? Allow your mind to roam freely around your experience of cats, writing down whatever emerges, without censoring it.

If you can't come up with any associations at all, ask yourself how you would describe a cat to an alien who's just arrived from another planet and has no idea of what a cat is or how it behaves. As you force yourself to look at this familiar creature with fresh eyes, you may suddenly find that you have hit upon the significance of the cat in your dream, as if by magic. If the image you are exploring is an object, you will need to tell your visitor what it does and how it works.

Amplification

This process will help you to bring the symbol fully alive so that it becomes a part of you, not just something you remember from a dream. There are many ways of amplifying an image but here are three I find especially useful.

Artwork

You don't have to be a great artist to paint or draw scenes and symbols from your dreams. It's fine to use stick figures for people and animals, and you don't need to reproduce an exact likeness of an object. What matters is to notice details. Does the dream animal have feet or is it flying around in the air? Do some people in the scene look much bigger than others? What does that say about my attitude to them? How is this relevant to a current situation? Some people prefer to make models of symbols, using substances that are easy to work with, like plasticine.

Movement

The characters and images in your dream bring messages from your inner world. If you can embody the messenger, you are more likely to understand the message. Let's see how this works in respect of the dream cat.

If you're agile enough, get down on all fours and allow yourself to feel cat-like. As you shake off your inhibitions, you will start moving more freely. You may find sounds emerging spontaneously, so that you find yourself purring or, if the cat in your dream was angry, hissing and flexing your claws. Now try walking around or lying down. How would it feel to come stalking into a room, demanding to be fed? If you're elderly or disabled, you can try this exercise sitting down, perhaps closing your eyes as you try to identify with the cat and make any movements that you can.

You can use movement in this way to explore the significance of any dream image.

Re-telling the dream

Another way of working with the characters in your dream is to re-tell it from their perspective. Supposing, for instance, that you identify with the cat in the dream and tell the story from its point of view, not yours. Notice how it feels about you and why. Is it trying to tell or show you something you need to know?

I recommend that you practise working with the images in your dream, even if I have discussed them in Part two. If I haven't included a symbol you need to know about then Association and Amplification will usually reveal its meaning. Sometimes though, a dream just doesn't seem to make sense, despite your best efforts. In this case, your unconscious mind will continue sending you dreams that carry the same message until the meaning becomes clear. This is why it's important to keep a record of your dreams. Eventually, you will be able to look back and understand the significance of many that made no sense at the time.

Now that you are equipped with some basic skills you are ready to start bringing your dreams alive.

Common dream themes

Anxiety dreams

Some researchers believe that anxiety dreams reflect a time when our ancestors were constantly threatened by danger from predators and other environmental factors. You will never be attacked by a sabre-toothed tiger, but if you are the object of savage criticism by your boss those ancient feelings of fear for your survival may be triggered deep within your unconscious mind and be reflected in your dreams.

Many anxiety dreams carry a message that your attitude to someone or something is unrealistic, or that you are heading in the wrong direction. If the dream keeps recurring, it's a sure sign that you have unfinished 'emotional business' to resolve.

Here are some of the most common anxiety dreams, each of which has several potential meanings. The correct interpretation is the one that most accurately mirrors your inmost feelings about yourself and your situation.

Being naked in public

Possible meanings

You dream you are in a public place when you suddenly realize you are naked. Although many people feel shame, embarrassment or horror in the dream, others are untroubled about being exposed to public gaze.

The dream usually indicates that you feel intensely vulnerable in some area of your life. It may be that a relationship has stripped away your defences, leaving you emotionally exposed. Perhaps you feel uncomfortable about an occasion when you revealed more of yourself than you had really wanted. Sometimes the dream suggests that you haven't yet found a suitable role in life.

If the dream is set in your office, it can signify underlying feelings of inadequacy about your work. You may be harbouring a fear that others will realize you are not as capable as they think.

Questions to ask yourself – and what to do when the answer is 'yes'

Do I feel emotionally susceptible?
● It may be that you have taken the role of victim in a relationship, so the dream is alerting you to the need to armour yourself. However, it's also possible that you are feeling defenceless because the other person is seeing you just as you are. If you usually hide behind a barrier, this can feel uncomfortable. Yet being loved for who you are is the basis of emotional healing and may be exactly what you need.

Am I worried that I may have revealed too much of myself?
● Perhaps you're usually a little too reticent, so that what you said or did wasn't nearly as explicit as you fear. Although it would be wise to watch for possible consequences your fears are likely to prove groundless.

Am I trying to find a suitable role in life?
● Unless you're lucky enough to have a vocation it can be difficult to find your niche in life. I suggest you seek advice from a careers counsellor.

Am I worried about my ability to do my job properly?
● If you are struggling with some aspect of your job, it would be best to ask for help or further training. Perhaps, though, you need to give yourself more credit for your abilities. You may be magnifying your shortcomings at the expense of your confidence. Could it be that you have unrealistically high expectations of yourself?

A dream where you don't mind baring all implies a lack of self-consciousness.

Being lost

Possible meanings

You dream that you are lost, desperately trying to find your way home. No matter which direction you take, you never manage to find the right road and nobody you meet can help you. Often this dream indicates that you want a more fulfilling job or a different lifestyle but you have no idea how to proceed.

If you come to a crossroads and don't know which way to take, it may mean that in waking life you are faced with several choices. You have to make a decision but don't know what to base it on.

Your destination sometimes provides a clue to the meaning of the dream. Perhaps you are trying to get back to a place where you used to have happy times. This suggests that your current lifestyle is unsatisfactory. If you are looking for a place you associate with your youth the dream implies concerns about growing older.

Being lost in a place that feels dangerous reflects feelings of unease about a current situation. The dream is a warning that someone or something is posing a threat to your well-being.

Dreams about being lost have special significance if you're middle-aged or elderly. The further you progress along your journey through life, the more essential it becomes to reassess your values and your priorities. Otherwise the more spiritual side of your nature remains unfulfilled so that, at a deeper level, you feel 'lost'.

**Questions to ask yourself –
and what to do when the answer is 'yes'**

Do I feel unfulfilled?
● If you find your job meaningless, career counselling could help you to identify both your innate abilities and the skills you've acquired through experience. It would also galvanize you into finding a more satisfying way of using them. If you need to reassess your entire lifestyle, you could benefit from the services of a life coach.

Am I faced with several choices?
● Your dilemma is offering you the chance to sort out your priorities, consulting your heart as well as your head. What do you most want from life? Which of the available choices would be most likely to help you get it? If you still feel confused, then why not follow a path that will make you feel glad to be alive?

Do I tend to live in the past?

● The more you cling to the past, the less meaningful your life will seem. You need to find a way of rekindling your enthusiasm, perhaps by injecting some fresh stimulus into your life. This could mean finding the courage to do something you've always longed to do but lacked the confidence to try.

Do I long to find my 'spiritual home'?

● Your dream is urging you to embark on a quest for self-knowledge and find a more authentic way of being. This means turning your attention within, perhaps through meditation or prayer. Spiritual counselling or psychotherapy can also help you to get in touch with your inner world and find your 'inner home', a state in which you feel emotionally and spiritually fulfilled.

Are you confused about which direction to take in your waking life?

Being pursued

You may be running from something you need to come to terms with.

Possible meanings

You are frantically running away from an unseen pursuer or perhaps a crowd of people. Yet you always wake up before you are caught.

An unknown pursuer often represents an inner force that you are reluctant to acknowledge but which is determined to become a part of your life. The more you try to run from it the more threatening it feels. You therefore need to turn and confront it. When you do you may find that something you assumed was hostile is in fact an ally. The pursuer may symbolize unused abilities or unresolved emotional issues.

Whatever is chasing you could be an unfriendly figure that embodies a situation you feel threatened by in waking life, like an illness, problems at work or difficulties in a relationship. It could also signify a negative aspect of your nature, usually a harsh inner critic that stops you from feeling at peace with yourself.

Being chased by someone you know may mean you are harbouring hostile feelings towards this person that you need to resolve.

Crowds of people who are pursuing you often symbolize the demands you make on yourself in an effort to please others.

Questions to ask yourself –
and what to do when the answer is 'yes'

What am I so desperate to avoid?
● Imagine confronting and holding a conversation with your pursuer. What do they want from you? What does your situation look like from their point of view? Could they represent an aspect of yourself you need to develop? This could introduce a new dimension into your life.

Is an aspect of my own nature undermining me?
● By running from this inner tyrant you are allowing it to have power over you. It can only do so, though, for as long as you believe that you cannot, or dare not, resist it. Standing up to it will bolster your confidence and enable you to take a bolder approach to challenges in your waking life.

Do I tend to put myself out too much for others?
● The dream is encouraging you to be more discriminating in the way you use your time. It's good to help others, but unwise to identify so completely with their needs that you underestimate your own.

Bomb

Possible meanings

A dream about a bomb can sometimes be triggered by a deeply disturbing experience in your waking life. Otherwise, your dream is trying to alert you to a potentially explosive situation. You may need to face up to feelings you have been suppressing before they overpower you and create havoc. If there is ongoing conflict in some area of your life, you could be toying with the idea of dropping a bombshell in an attempt to resolve it, once and for all.

Questions to ask yourself –
and what to do when the answer is 'yes'

Have I been thrown off balance by a traumatic event?
● Under these circumstances, healing ultimately comes with the passage of time. If you do your best to adjust to the new circumstances, you will emerge from your experience with wisdom you might not otherwise have gained.

Am I repressing some powerful feelings?
● Your dream is urging you to try and resolve the situation before you blow a fuse. If you don't know how to go about it, consider confiding in a friend or a member of your family. If this is impossible, then it would be best to seek professional help.

Would I secretly like to say or do something explosive?
● Whilst you may have good reason to feel as you do, cultivating a sense of being hard done by can only make matters worse. If you want your circumstances to change, you must be first willing to change your attitude. Can you see how you have actually helped to create this situation? This means that you are actually more powerful than you think you are. Claiming that power and using it more wisely is the key to success.

If you've had a sudden big shock, you may dream of a bomb explosion.

Drowning

Possible meanings

Since water is a metaphor for feelings, a dream about drowning usually means that you are afraid of being overwhelmed by powerful emotions. If an intense relationship of yours is going wrong, for instance, you may be experiencing a sinking feeling in your waking life that is subsequently reflected in your dream.

If your relationships are not the issue, your dream could reflect any situation where you feel you've lost control. Perhaps you are finding it difficult to keep your head above water financially, or feeling out of your depth in some other area of your life.

Maybe you have taken on so many responsibilities that you are inundated with demands on your time and energy.

A dream about drowning can sometimes reflect a health challenge. If you suffer from water retention, the dream could be a warning that your condition is getting worse. It would be wise to see your doctor as a precautionary measure.

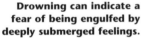

Drowning can indicate a fear of being engulfed by deeply submerged feelings.

Questions to ask yourself – and what to do when the answer is 'yes'

Am I afraid of being overwhelmed by my feelings?
● You need emotional support, so don't hesitate to discuss your feelings with someone whose calm judgment you respect. Talking things through may not alter the situation, but will help you to be more objective about it.

Am I in a situation that I feel helpless to control?
● I suggest you seek appropriate advice without delay. Whether you need a relationship counsellor, a financial adviser or another source of professional help, taking this initial step will help you to feel more in charge.

Am I inundated with demands on my time and energy?
● Your dream is challenging you to learn to say 'no', kindly but firmly. Could you delegate some of your responsibilities? If the thought fills you with horror, you may be trying too hard to control too many aspects of your life and need to sort out your priorities.

Examinations

Possible meanings

You are about to take an exam when you realize that you've done no revision and won't be able to answer any of the questions. If exams are looming in waking life, your dream could be warning you to work harder.

Usually the dream reflects a situation in your waking life in which you feel you are being tested. Whether you are facing a challenge at work or difficulties in a relationship, you are harbouring a fear of failing to make the grade. If you passed all your exams years ago, your dream may imply that, despite all the evidence to the contrary, you've never quite believed in your ability to succeed. You therefore have this kind of dream whenever you are involved in a situation that triggers your insecurities.

Perhaps you are taking an exam in a subject you've never studied. This can mean that you feel ill-equipped to deal with a situation you've never met before, as you have no previous experience to draw on. More often though the dream suggests a tendency to set yourself impossibly high standards, then criticize yourself for falling short of them.

Questions to ask yourself – and what to do when the answer is 'yes'

Am I worried that I'm failing to meet other people's expectations?
● Your dream suggests that your real problem is your habit of judging yourself and finding yourself wanting. You then automatically expect others to do the same. You can transform this no-win situation by cultivating a kinder more respectful attitude to yourself.

Do I find it hard to accept success?
● Many talented, hard-working people secretly feel they don't really deserve their success. A good way of counteracting this is to make a list of everything you've achieved since you first learnt to walk and talk. By the time you have acknowledged several hundred achievements, you will have begun to realize just how accomplished you are.

Do I expect too much of myself?
● The dream is encouraging you to be less self-critical. Cultivate a more relaxed acceptance of your own best efforts and avoid setting yourself standards that are unrealistically high. Try to see life as a process or a journey to be explored, not a test to be endured.

Exams show others your capabilities. Are you worried you won't measure up?

Falling from a height

Fear of falling in a dream can suggest concerns about loss of status.

Possible meanings

Your dream could imply that you lack emotional support, or that you need to learn to stand on your own two feet. However, it may also reflect insecurities about your status. If financial pressures have forced you into taking a job for which you are over-qualified, for instance, you may feel you have 'come down in the world'.

The dream can also imply that you are out of touch with reality. Perhaps you have too high an opinion of your abilities. Maybe you tend to live in a fantasy world of grandiose schemes and unrealistic expectations. Lofty aims mean little unless you are prepared to work at realizing your ambitions. Your dream is trying to shock you into coming down to earth.

You can also have a dream like this if you've discovered that someone or something is not as you had been led to believe.

Questions to ask yourself – and what to do when the answer is 'yes'

Do I lack emotional support?
● Have you, in fact, asked for help? If you are expecting someone to read your mind you will probably be disappointed. The dream is encouraging you to be more direct and make your needs known.

Am I concerned about a loss of status?
● Since our culture places great emphasis on status, it would be good to decide what worries you more, your actual loss of standing or other people's reactions to your position. Your dream is urging you to realize that it's who you are that matters, not what you do.

Do I need to adopt a more realistic perspective?
● Your dream is a message about the need to accept your limitations as well as your strengths. You could find it helpful to pursue activities that put you in touch with nature, like gardening or rambling. The dream may also be warning you that nurturing grandiose ideas is harming your relationships. Try to focus more on others and less on yourself.

Am I feeling let down?
● If you have been duped, it would be easy to become cynical or wallow in self-pity. Neither attitude, though, will enhance your life. I suggest you make a decision to learn from your experience and then to move on, knowing that you are now a little wiser.

Fire

Possible meanings

Fire often represents 'hot' emotions like rage or sexual passion. If the fire is out of control, your dream could be warning you about the dangers of being involved in a situation that's too hot to handle. Perhaps you are incandescent with rage or in danger of being consumed by a destructive desire. The dream may also reflect a burning issue you need to resolve.

A dream in which your house is on fire can signify a high temperature, inflammation in some part of your body or raised blood pressure.

Fire is a traditional symbol of transformation and purification, so if you are suffering in your waking life, the message could be that you are undergoing a baptism of fire. Something old or worn out is being burned away so that new developments can arise.

Questions to ask yourself – and what to do when the answer is 'yes'

Am I involved in a potentially explosive situation?
● If you are passionately attracted to someone other than your partner, your dream could be urging you to consider the damaging consequences of taking this further. Perhaps you are secretly enjoying the drama, in which case it would be much wiser to find an alternative way of injecting excitement into your life.

Am I feeling overwhelmed by intense feelings?
● You may feel unable to express your pent-up emotions in case they create havoc. If the problem is that you are being treated unjustly, why not ask someone you trust to act as an intermediary? Otherwise, a tried and tested therapeutic way of letting off steam is to beat a cushion as though it's the person or situation you find so frustrating.

Am I overdue for a health check?
● One of the healing functions of dreams is to let you know when something is physically amiss. Your dream is therefore urging you to take responsibility for your health.

Am I upset about the way things are changing?
● If a caterpillar resisted change, it would never become a beautiful butterfly. Rest assured that your life is being transformed for the better. You can further the process by identifying negative attitudes or limiting beliefs that are stopping you from fulfilling your potential.

Fire can represent passion that is all-consuming and uncontrolled.

Keeping out intruders

Possible meanings

You are alone in the house. Outside, a burglar is prowling around, looking for a way in. Terrified, you rush from room to room, locking all the doors and windows, but they keep on coming unfastened.

A dream like this can mean that somebody in your waking life is getting too close for comfort. More commonly, the intruder symbolizes an aspect of your own nature with which you do not normally identify.

If you try to cry out for help but cannot make a sound, the dream may relate to a situation that is threatening your security. Yet you feel powerless to do anything about it.

Since a house symbolizes the person you feel you truly are, your dream could also imply that you are trying to protect your sense of self from being disturbed by something new or unfamiliar. You are therefore suppressing something you secretly want to do or be.

**Questions to ask yourself –
and what to do when the answer is 'yes'**

Is someone intruding on my personal space?
● If this person doesn't respond to tactful hints, but you don't want to upset them, perhaps you could ask a mutual friend to explain your feelings. However, if you tend to keep people at a distance your dream could be urging you to let down your guard and discover the joys of intimacy.

Do I need to celebrate a side of myself I usually repress?
● Constantly trying to disown something that is an essential part of your personality creates stress. Relax those rigid boundaries you have set around yourself. They are like a psychic straitjacket, depriving you of the freedom to be who you are. Life will be more joyful when you take it off.

Do I feel unable to deal with a situation that's making me feel insecure?
● If you could speak with a voice of authority the situation would seem less daunting. You could consider assertiveness training or counselling. You may benefit from taking classes in public speaking or drama. Above all you need to believe in yourself.

Am I stopping myself from fulfilling a secret desire?
● The more your fearful side insists on protecting your defences, the more your adventurous side feels like a dangerous outsider prowling around the periphery of your mind. Your dream is urging you to let it in.

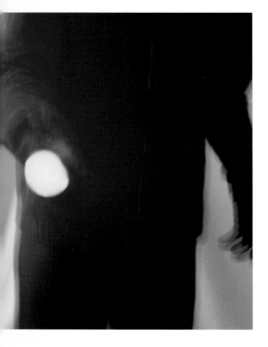

An intruder can personify a part of yourself that you have tried hard to repress.

Killing someone

Possible meanings

You realize you've killed someone. You didn't mean to do it and you're not sure how it happened. Now you're terrified that you're going to be found out.

This unsettling nightmare is an urgent wake-up call. It usually means that you've tried to disown or failed to develop an important aspect of your own nature. Your efforts have been so successful that it's now as good as dead. In my experience, people who have this dream often appear more passive and obliging than they actually are. They secretly fear that their power, once unleashed, could prove lethal.

Killing someone may show a desire to destroy the power they have over you.

To enjoy the healing benefits of the dream, it's important to understand what the dead body represents. If it's someone you know, then he or she may have a quality that you secretly admire but don't dare to demonstrate in your own life.

If the 'victim' is a close friend or a member of your family, your dream could suggest that you are harbouring feelings of hatred which you don't want to acknowledge, even to yourself. An alternative meaning is that you are too closely identified with this person, and subconsciously want to 'kill off' the relationship in order to gain your independence.

Questions to ask yourself – and what to do when the answer is 'yes'

Have I tried to 'kill off' a part of myself that I'm afraid to reveal?
● Imagine how you would feel if you were to embody this quality. Would you stand taller, move more purposefully, or speak more authoritatively? You are now being more fully yourself. From this position, how would you relate to others?

Am I harbouring murderous feelings towards someone?
● It's essential to find a way of expressing your feelings harmlessly. You could try drawing or painting them. If you need a more physical outlet, you can try beating up a cushion or working off your feelings through strenuous exercise. I also recommend that you pray for the ability to forgive this person – even if you are not especially religious.

Could I be too dependent on someone?
● The best relationships are those between people who feel free to be themselves rather than being joined at the hip. Your dream is therefore encouraging you to assert your right to be who you are.

Teeth are falling out

Possible meanings

Are you overdue for a visit to the dentist? If not, your dream has one of several symbolic meanings.

Since teeth are essential for chewing food, they can symbolize your 'bite on life', the degree to which you feel forceful or decisive. Loose teeth may therefore indicate the need for you to have a more positive attitude. Do you need to 'get your teeth' into something? Or maybe you need to 'chew things over' with somebody who can help you to cope more effectively. Weak or wobbly teeth can also imply that you have bitten off more than you can chew.

Losing your teeth often represents a concern about how you appear to others. Is there a situation in which you feel you have failed to project a good self-image?

Since babies have no teeth, your dream may be warning you about an immature attitude. An alternative interpretation is based on the fact that losing your teeth has, until recently, been associated with old age. In this case, the dream indicates a hidden fear of growing older.

Teeth have traditionally been compared to battlements guarding the entrance to our private, inner world. Losing them can therefore represent a fear of letting down your defences and exposing your true feelings.

**Questions to ask yourself –
and what to do when the answer is 'yes'**

Do I find it hard to make decisions?
● You may find it beneficial to invest in a life coach or a course of assertiveness training. Creative work could also be helpful, as it involves a constant decision-making process.

Am I too concerned about what other people think of me?
● Please bear in mind that you are probably more critical of yourself than anyone else is of you. Your dream is inviting you to cultivate a kinder, warmer attitude towards yourself, as though you were your own best friend. If you are at ease with yourself, you are bound to project a positive self-image.

Am I behaving in an immature way?
● It's time to grow up and take responsibility for yourself. If you're not sure how, a counsellor or therapist would be able to help you.

Am I worried about growing older?

● Focus on the positive side of growing old. You're so much more experienced and wiser, too. Maybe you've slowed down a little, but maybe by not rushing so much you can appreciate all those things that you once passed by and, in your haste, ignored.

Do I need the courage to reveal my true feelings?

● This may feel scary, but rest assured that a deeper and wiser part of you knows it's in your own best interests. If you need support, why not ask a sympathetic friend or relative to help you?

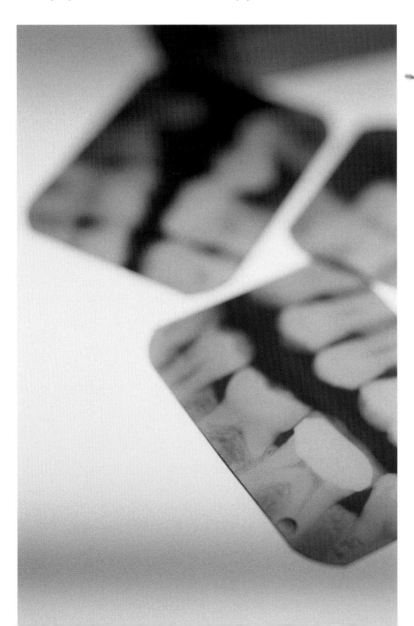

Problems with teeth can reflect anxiety about the image you present to others.

Performance

Possible meanings

You dream you are about to go on stage when, to your horror, you realize you have forgotten your lines or your moves.

If you are due to take part in a performance in your waking life, the dream may simply be a form of stage fright or a message about the need for further preparation.

Otherwise, dreams like this usually reflect a concern about your performance on the stage of life. Perhaps you lack confidence, or have an underlying fear of failing to meet other people's standards. This is often the case if, as a child, you were under pressure to conform to parental or other expectations. Your lack of preparation in the dream reflects a subconscious determination to rebel against the pressure to fit in with what others want.

In one version of this dream, you aren't meant to be in the show and have no idea what you're supposed to do. Yet everyone expects you to know your role. This suggests that in waking life you try too hard to meet other people's needs.

Do you feel unprepared to face a challenge in your waking life?

Questions to ask yourself – and what to do when the answer is 'yes'

Do I lack confidence?
● Counselling or drama therapy could be helpful. Otherwise, I suggest you try one of the many recorded self-hypnosis programmes now widely available. You could also benefit from taking a class in something you've always wanted to do. The more skilful you become, the more confident you will feel.

Am I worried about living up to other people's expectations?
● Your dream is a message that subconsciously you are tired of feeling obliged to conform. It's now time to stop taking your cue from others and start learning to dance to your own individual tune.

Do I tend to be too accommodating?
● Your dream is encouraging you to step out from behind the scenes. You may not always want to be in the spotlight, but you do need to reveal some important aspects of your personality that have been marginalized. You might find it helpful to imagine that you have written a play. Which role would you most like to take? How can you incorporate more of this character's qualities into your daily life?

Problems with journeys

Failure to make progress could be a message that your destiny lies elsewhere.

Possible meanings

You arrive at the airport, only to find that you have left your passport and tickets behind. Or you're on holiday when you suddenly realize it's time to leave and you've done no packing.

People who have dreams like these are often extremely efficient in waking life and try to leave nothing to chance. Whilst it's wonderful to have great organizational ability, it's also important to leave room in your life for joyous spontaneity. Your dream may therefore be a cry for recognition from a part of you that no longer wants to be driven by the need to cope efficiently with every eventuality.

Waiting for a bus or a train that never arrives suggests that you are being left behind in an area of life where you want to accomplish something. Somehow you never seem to get the opportunity you need.

A bus or train that's bound for the wrong destination may reflect the fact that something just isn't going your way. Alternatively, the dream can be a message about the need to reconsider a goal you've set yourself. Sometimes this dream indicates an inner conflict between a wish to stay within your familiar 'comfort zone' and a need to meet new challenges.

The discussion in the section on 'Journeys' (see pages 48–57) offers further clues to the precise meaning of your dream.

Questions to ask yourself – and what to do when the answer is 'yes'

Do I pride myself on being orderly and methodical?
● Your dream is intuiting you to take a holiday from your need to feel constantly in control. You would benefit from allowing yourself to relax a little and allow the principle of serendipity to enrich your life.

Am I waiting for an opportunity that never seems to materialize?
● Instead of hoping that something will turn up, you need to find ways of creating opportunities for yourself. I suggest you begin by getting in touch with anybody you think may be able to help you.

Do I tend to stick with what I know?
● You will make more of your life if you try to see it as a journey of exploration. You cannot know the nature of your ultimate destination in advance but you certainly won't get there by staying put. Your dream is alerting you to the benefits of cultivating a more adventurous outlook.

Sentenced to death

Being senetenced to death in a dream often signifies a need for drastic change.

Possible meanings

Dreams in which you are sentenced to death or about to be shot can have several different symbolic meanings. Your dream may be urging you to recognize the need for total transformation in some area of your life. Being shot in the head implies that it's essential to think about something in a completely different way.

Often, a dream like this indicates that you have sustained a severe emotional and psychological shock, from which you have not yet recovered. An alternative meaning is that you are the target of somebody's aggression or have an underlying sense of being constantly 'under fire'.

Occasionally, the dream can reflect feelings of despair about a situation that seems to threaten your very existence.

Questions to ask yourself – and what to do when the answer is 'yes'

Does some area of my life need to undergo radical change?
● It's time to summon up your courage and set the process in motion. This may mean handing in your notice, ending your relationship or putting your house on the market. Your dream is warning you against allowing fear of the unknown to deter you from making overdue changes in your lifestyle.

Do I need a complete change of perspective about who and what I am?
● Your dream suggests that a part of you has to 'die' so that you are free to develop your true self and enjoy greater fulfilment. It's time to 'get shot of' outdated beliefs about yourself. Such radical change is best undertaken with the help of a therapist.

Am I the target of someone's hostility?
● I recommend that you seek an explanation for this person's animosity, perhaps with the support of somebody you can trust to facilitate the encounter. If you're being bullied at work, it would be best to discuss the problem with the Human Resources department.

Am I in a situation that feels life-threatening?
● Your dream is warning you to get out of the firing line. This could mean taking drastic action so please don't hesitate to seek help from the most appropriate source.

Vampire

Possible meanings

If you find that being with somebody leaves you feeling physically or emotionally drained, he or she may appear in your dream in the guise of a vampire. Sometimes, though, the vampire symbolizes a destructive part of your own nature, such as a tendency to indulge in negative thoughts that sap your energy and make you depressed.

A dream of a vampire could also be a message that you are too needy or greedy for love, attention or sex.

Since vampires are associated with young women, they sometimes appear in the dreams of teenage girls who are starting to explore their sexuality. In a man's dream, a vampire can personify fear of being devoured by a woman.

Questions to ask yourself – and what to do when the answer is 'yes'

Is somebody I know draining me?
● For a while, at least, you may have to distance yourself from this person. If you can, it would be good to explain what you are doing and why, so that they have an opportunity to reflect on their behaviour.

Am I being eaten up by negative thoughts?
● A course of counselling, or treatment from a spiritual healer, could help to change your outlook. Otherwise, you could try listening to a self-hypnosis recording that induces a positive frame of mind.

Am I too demanding or emotionally dependent?
● Until you discover what makes your life meaningful, you're unlikely to enjoy satisfactory relationships. Your dream is a wake-up call to start exploring your abilities and cultivating your interests.

As a teenage girl, am I thinking of having sex for the first time?
● Losing your virginity is a major rite of passage for which you need to be emotionally prepared. The dream may therefore be warning you against being drawn into a situation over which you have no control.

As a man, am I afraid of being overwhelmed by a woman?
● This is a fear that lurks deep within many a masculine psyche. If it's stopping you from having a fulfilling relationship, you may need to consider seeking professional help.

This may be a warning against allowing someone to have power over you.

Dream people

Other people in a dream generally symbolize aspects of yourself that you are unaware of or prefer not to recognize. A person of the same sex personifies qualities that you have repressed and need to incorporate into your personality. Someone of the opposite sex embodies the hidden masculine or feminine side of your nature. Being on good terms with your inner man or woman helps you to enjoy more fulfilling relationships.

Anybody you've ever met can appear in a dream. Even somebody you haven't seen for years may represent the element of healing needed in a current relationship. Dreams featuring a close friend or relative need special attention. He or she could symbolize a part of your self. However, the dream is more likely to reveal an aspect of this person that you have overlooked, or to say something about your relationship.

This section introduces you to some characters who appear regularly in dreams.

Monarchs and presidents

Possible meanings

In ancient times, kings and queens were considered sacred. Although we no longer revere them in this way, they still have a hold on our collective imagination. This is why you can have dreams about royals even if you don't live in a monarchy. Symbolically speaking, a president fulfils a similar role.

A king or president can represent your father, your boss or another 'alpha male'. Your dream could reflect your relationship with him or your attitude to masculine power and authority in general.

A king was traditionally expected to embody the highest ideals of the culture he ruled over. He can therefore symbolize your inmost self, the deeper, wiser part of you that guides your destiny and inspires you to become the person you are meant to be.

A queen personifies mature feminine strength and dignity, as well as the feminine values of relationship and feeling. She may also symbolize your mother, or a woman who occupies a position of authority.

If the monarch or president is old or ill, your dream is inviting you to reappraise your values. A more forward-looking attitude is the key to resolving a current difficulty.

The trappings of monarchy can signify nobility of spirit.

**Questions to ask yourself –
and what to do when the answer is 'yes'**

Am I at loggerheads with an authority figure?
● When you were a child, you may have resented the power that your father or another significant adult had over you. It's time to come to terms with those old, unresolved feelings. Their negative influence on your behaviour towards people in positions of authority is creating unnecessary problems.

Do I need to claim my own authority?
● Are you confusing 'authority' with its negative manifestation 'authoritarian'? If you stand up for your feelings and values, others will respect your integrity even if they disagree. If there is a situation in which you need to take the role of leader, it would be irresponsible not to do so.

Do I need to develop my relationship skills?
You could begin by listening more carefully to others and encouraging them to express their feelings. If you find it hard to know what your own feelings are you could benefit from consulting a counsellor.

Celebrities

Possible meanings

You are having a relationship with a celebrity and feel proud that he or she has singled you out for attention. If you're a teenager, your dream could simply reflect a current crush, but if you're an older fan, it may be warning you against hero-worship. More often, though, the dream is compensating for a lack of excitement in a humdrum existence. It can also reflect a desire for recognition, fame or power.

There is one further interpretation. Although its content may be erotic, the actual meaning of your dream could have more to do with fulfilment of a different kind. You are not living up to your potential, so the star personifies something that you know in your heart you could be.

Dreaming of a celebrity can reflect a desire to be considered special.

Questions to ask yourself – and what to do when the answer is 'yes'

Am I in my teens?
● Having a crush on a celebrity is a normal phase of your emotional development. With the advent of a 'real-life' romance, you'll find these dreams will stop.

Am I an adult fan of the star?
● A charismatic figure of the opposite sex usually represents your ideal man or woman. Yet if you subconsciously endow somebody with godlike status, your own role, by implication, is that of worshipper. Your dream may therefore indicate a tendency to put yourself down. It is inviting you to form an exciting new relationship ... with your own greatness.

Do I feel bored?
● Life is only boring if you let it get that way. Try to vary your daily routine. Even something as simple as going for a walk instead of slumping in front of the television could help you to feel more alive.

Am I living below my true capacity?
● The celebrity represents a powerful, talented but hitherto dormant aspect of your own nature that you need to awaken. Start by making a list of all the qualities you most admire about this person. Now go through the list, crossing out his or her name and substituting your own. If you can't believe what you read, I suspect you are too cynical about yourself and your potential.

Friends

Possible meanings

If you are having problems with a friend in waking life, your dream may simply reflect the issues involved.

Otherwise, your friend has a symbolic meaning. We often choose as friends people who have qualities that we would secretly like to exhibit, but feel we dare not, or cannot. In your dream, your friend therefore personifies a suppressed side of yourself.

Perhaps your dream features someone you used to be friendly with but haven't seen for years. Again, he or she may represent an aspect of your own nature. However, if you parted on bad terms, or shared hopes and dreams that were never fulfilled, the dream could say something about the need to heal your memories.

Questions to ask yourself –
and what to do when the answer is 'yes'

Does my friend have qualities I admire or envy?

● You may see your friend as being sexier, wittier, more successful or ruthless than you. Whatever he or she represents, though, your dream is a message that you too can cultivate these qualities – if that is what you really want. It can be easier to settle for admiring someone else's greatness than to work at developing your own. Your dream is challenging you to become more of who you are.

Did an old friendship end in an unsatisfactory way?

● Your dream could reflect a sudden impulse to get in touch with your friend and see if you can mend your relationship. Otherwise, the message is that you need to let go of any feelings of anger, guilt or regret you are still harbouring. If you don't, they could make you over-react to problems you may have in current friendships.

Friends usually represent parts of your personality you need to 'befriend'.

Husbands and wives

Possible meanings

A dream about your husband or wife often reflects current issues in your relationship.

Your spouse personifies the masculine or feminine side of your own nature. This can appear in dreams as a positive or negative figure. For instance, your husband could symbolize logic or sarcasm, assertiveness or aggression, whether or not he actually demonstrates these qualities in waking life. He may do – but it's also possible that what you see in him is something you need to recognize within yourself.

Your wife can represent qualities like sensitivity or moodiness, empathy or possessiveness. Your dream is using her as a symbol in order to show you a side of yourself of which you are perhaps unaware.

If you are divorced, dreaming that you are back with your ex could imply that you haven't yet let go of the hopes and dreams you once had for your marriage. It can also mean you are still harbouring feelings like anger or bitterness towards your ex.

A dream in which your husband or wife goes off with someone else often has no basis in reality. In this case, it reflects insecurities that you need to keep in check or, better still, deal with before they corrode the relationship. If, though, the dream does reflect a real-life situation, time may be the only real healer. Many people take years to recover from a betrayal of trust.

Questions to ask yourself – and what to do when the answer is 'yes'

Do I need to confront problems in my marriage?
● It looks as though you will have to bring some uncomfortable feelings out into the open. If you find it hard to communicate with your spouse, I highly recommend you consult a marriage guidance counsellor. You may have to overcome some inhibitions before you can speak freely, but this is the only way of restoring harmony to your relationship.

Does my spouse have characteristics I dislike?
● It's easier to see someone else's shortcomings than to recognize our own. Your dream may be trying to show you that the qualities you dislike in your spouse correspond to a part of your own personality. You may have to grapple with your pride before you can accept this but the effect on your marriage could be magical.

Do I still have strong feelings about my ex?

● Your dream is urging you to accept reality, forgive and forget. Unless you do, you risk jeopardizing your chances of finding happiness with somebody else.

Do I feel insecure despite having a loving, faithful partner?

● I highly recommend that you seek professional help to tackle feelings that may have developed long ago, maybe in your childhood. Otherwise they could eventually undermine your marriage.

A dream about your spouse may reflect hidden conflicts between you.

Children

Possible meanings

Your dream may be commenting on your relationship with a child. For instance, if you believe that a loving parent never shows anger, your suppressed feelings may emerge in a dream about having a furious argument with your child. More symbolically, the dream could suggest that you have an immature attitude in some area of your waking life.

A little boy can personify the spirit of adventure. Do you secretly want to start a new project, explore your creativity, or take a course? A young girl represents developments within your feminine, more sensitive side. With 'her' help, you can enjoy better relationships.

The child's age is often a clue to the dream's meaning. Supposing he or she is eight-years-old. Has a current situation triggered memories of something that was happening in your life when you were that age? It's also possible that the dream relates to something that started eight years ago, perhaps a relationship or project, or even a change of attitude.

A very young child sometimes signifies a new phase of life. If you're in your middle years, the dream is encouraging you to let go of the past and embrace the joys and privileges of your new status as a mature person.

A child can personify a side of you that is playful and spontaneous.

Questions to ask yourself – and what to do when the answer is 'yes'

Do I try to hide feelings like anger from my child?
● Try to find a loving but firm way of expressing your feelings more openly. Your child will respect the fact that you are being truthful.

Is there a situation in which I'm being childish?
● You are allowing yourself to be driven by an immature side of your nature, such as the need to have your own way. The dream is urging you to practise self-discipline.

Do I find it hard to be spontaneous?
● You probably worry too much about how others will react to you. If you allow the voice of the 'child within' to speak, people will sense that you are being authentic and will respect your views.

Do I need to resolve feelings I've been harbouring since my childhood?
Your dream is urging you to heal old wounds, so that you are free to embrace life more fully. As you may need to release some powerful emotions, it would be best to seek professional help.

Parents

Possible meanings

The ability to see your parents as people in their own right is a hallmark of maturity. Your dream may therefore be encouraging you to look at them with fresh eyes so that you develop a healthier relationship.

Your parent could also symbolize your partner. Subconsciously, we often look for partners whose personality reminds us of our mother or father. If you had a poor relationship with that parent, your dream may be warning you against recreating similar problems.

A father represents qualities like authority and the ability to provide for his family. If your father was tyrannical or irresponsible, your dream could indicate that you subconsciously expect all men to behave as he did.

Although mothers are traditionally associated with nurturing and protection, yours may have been neglectful or possessive. If so, your dream could reveal a deep-rooted distrust of women that you need to face up to, perhaps with professional help. Alternatively, you may be going through a difficult patch and subconsciously be longing to be mothered.

Sometimes a dream about parents is alerting you to the fact that you are repeating their patterns of parenting with your own children.

Questions to ask yourself – and what to do when the answer is 'yes'

Do I find it hard to think of my parents as people?

● Your dream is urging you to be more objective. How much do you know about your parents' lives? Knowing something of their history would help you to understand them better and could help to heal old wounds.

Does my partner remind me of one of my parents?

● Deep down, you may have chosen your partner in the hope that he or she would compensate for your parents' shortcomings. Your dream is trying to help you to recognize that your partner is a unique individual, not the embodiment of your own hopes and fears.

Am I repeating my parents' patterns with my own children?

● If your parents were controlling or overprotective, you may be relating in a similar way to your own children. It would be helpful to consider the way in which you use your power as a parent. Whilst you owe it to your children to give them clear boundaries, they also need to be given opportunities to develop their initiative.

Dreaming of your parents can reflect emotional issues that are unresolved.

Brothers and sisters

Possible meanings

Dreaming about your brother or sister could reflect a current problem in your relationship. Often it's the result of an issue that dates back to your childhood but has never been resolved.

As children, you may have been rivals for your parents' attention or approval. Perhaps your sibling was academically outstanding, artistically gifted or a natural at sports, and you felt inadequate by comparison. You could still be harbouring jealousy or a subconscious need to compete.

A sibling can also personify an aspect of yourself. In this case, a brother represents your more masculine, goal-oriented, competitive tendencies. Your sister may embody feminine characteristics like sensitivity and the desire to co-operate. A dream in which you are on bad terms with your sibling can therefore imply that you need to have a better relationship with this side of your own nature.

Perhaps your dream brother or sister is behaving in a way you find annoying. Whether or not this reflects their conduct in waking life, your dream may be asking you to recognize that you, too, are capable of behaving in a similar way.

Siblings tend to symbolize undeveloped aspects of your own personality.

Questions to ask yourself – and what to do when the answer is 'yes'

Have I always felt competitive with my brother or sister?

● Your dream suggests that, deep down, you are still affected by emotional wounds you sustained during childhood. A frank discussion with your sibling could help to heal them, setting you free to develop the potential you suppressed by your lack of faith in your own abilities.

Do I need to be on better terms with some aspect of myself?

Can you think of an occasion when you reacted in a similar way to the brother or sister in your dream? You may find it hard to accept this side of your nature, but it's in your own interests to be honest with yourself. Instead of disparaging this quality, try to think of ways in which it could be useful to you?

Am I more like my sibling than I care to admit?

● Recognizing characteristics in yourself that you dislike in others takes courage. If you can face up to your shortcomings though, your relationships will improve dramatically.

Sex

Possible meanings

You are having blissful, passionate sex with an ex-lover or colleague, a member of your family, or even an unknown person. Your dream could be compensating for a dull or non-existent sex-life. Otherwise your dream lover embodies a quality that you need to embrace. An erotic dream involving your boss, for instance, could reflect a desire for power or status.

Dreams about making love can also imply a need to connect with your own masculine or feminine side, regardless of your sexual persuasion. Same-sex encounters do not necessarily imply homosexuality. Often they suggest that important developments are taking place within your personality, leading you further along the road to wholeness.

A dream about sex with a parent or sibling could simply signify that your current partner shares similar characteristics. It may also indicate that in waking life someone is trying to make you do something against your better judgment. However, if your dream is a replay of abuse you actually suffered, I urge you to seek professional help.

A dream in which you discover your partner having sex with somebody else may reflect your own insecurities and bear no relation to reality. If you have good reason to suspect your partner is being unfaithful, describing your dream may be a way of bringing things out into the open.

Questions to ask yourself – and what to do when the answer is 'yes'

Do I need to develop my masculine side?
● Taking up a sport or a martial art could help you to become more focused or assertive. If you find it difficult to think clearly and logically, you could benefit from taking a class in a subject like philosophy or maths.

Do I need a closer relationship with my feminine nature?
● If you don't feel at ease in relationships, you could consider attending one of the many relevant workshops now widely available. Or you may prefer to join a drama group or take a dance class. Some people find that 'adopting' an elderly, lonely person is an unthreatening way of learning to express their feelings.

Is someone taking advantage of me?
● Your dream is urging you to learn the art of saying 'no'. Before long, you'll wonder how on earth you could have been so compliant!

Your dream lover may embody a part of your own nature, yet to be embraced.

Baby

Possible meanings

You suddenly remember that you have a baby and it's been weeks since you fed or changed her. To your relief, she seems fit and healthy. For an expectant mother, this is a classic anxiety dream reflecting your concerns about the responsibilities of motherhood.

In most dreams though, a baby symbolizes a new development in your life – so men too can have dreams like these. It may be that you have been offered a new opportunity, taken on a project or started a new relationship. Neglecting the baby implies that you're not giving this new situation the care and attention it deserves. It could also mean, though, that you're in a position to make a fresh start but doing nothing about it. In some dreams, a neglected baby personifies a vulnerable, sensitive side of yourself whose needs you have overlooked.

Finding a baby often suggests you are discovering hidden talents or abilities. If you've forgotten to feed it though, the message is that you need to put more energy into nurturing your newfound potential.

Perhaps you have a miraculous baby that can talk like an adult. This dream usually coincides with a period of significant inner growth when you are discovering new intellectual, emotional or spiritual capacities.

Women who are nearing the end of their reproductive years can dream about a baby if they are anxious about losing their fertility and yearn to have one last child. However, the dream could also signify the start of the next phase of life, with all its new possibilities.

Questions to ask yourself –
and what to do when the answer is 'yes'

Are new developments happening in my life?
● If you are neglecting the baby, the dream is alerting you to the need to nurture the new situation, so that you maximize its potential. This may involve further training, for instance, or seeking people who can help to further your aims. If the dream refers to a new relationship, you need to be aware that it won't take care of itself. You have to work at creating a solid basis of friendship.

Am I discovering new talents?
● If you are focusing on the needs of others at the expense of your own, you are now seriously short-changing yourself. Your dream is urging you to make time and space in your life to develop your abilities.

Am I a woman nearing the menopause?

● If you're feeling broody, you need to ask yourself some searching questions. Have you stopped to reflect on the advantages of maturity? You're probably more confident than before, less concerned about what others think. If your family is grown up, you now have the opportunity to focus on your inner life. Your longing for a baby may be disguising a deeper need to develop other aspects of your creativity that will bring you renewed optimism and vitality.

A baby can represent a new relationship that has great potential.

Witch

Possible meanings

Witches were originally wise women and healers, so if your dream features a benevolent witch, you can look forward to improvements in your physical or emotional well-being.

It's more likely, though, that the witch is a frightening, potentially destructive figure. Sometimes she reflects hidden feelings you may have about an overly possessive or manipulative mother. She can also symbolize a vindictive, controlling or jealous aspect of your own nature.

If you are a man, the witch in your dream may embody a secret fear of falling victim to a woman's power. You are therefore on bad terms with your own feminine, sensitive side, and tend to be sulky, defensive or resentful when you are confronted with problems in a relationship.

**Questions to ask yourself –
and what to do when the answer is 'yes'**

Do I have a difficult relationship with my mother?
● Assuming your mother is still alive, trying to reach a mutual under-standing would help to heal the relationship, even if you don't manage to resolve your problems entirely. It's up to you to take the first step. If your mother is unapproachable though, or has died, you may find it helpful to express your feelings by writing down a story about your relationship with her.

Do I try and control others?
● A wish for power over others often stems from a deep sense of inadequacy. Your dream is urging you to develop a stronger sense of your own worth. You could begin by channelling some of the energy that's currently focused on other people's activities into a creative pursuit. It doesn't matter what this is, as long as you enjoy the process of doing it for its own sake.

As a man, do I have difficulty getting close to women?
● If your relationships have been soured by your early experience of your mother, you need to address some deep-rooted fears. This is hard to do on your own and men are notoriously reluctant to seek counselling. I assure you, though, that if you can overcome your reservations and allow yourself to be helped, you will be rewarded with the ability to enjoy fulfilling relationships.

A witch suggests healing but also the destructive use of a feminine power.

Ghost

Possible meanings

A ghostly figure in a dream often represents feelings that continue to haunt you long after the event that initially triggered them. It could also symbolize a fantasy whose subtle but powerful influence stops you from facing up to reality.

Sometimes a ghost can signify a suppressed talent you have that's hovering around in the background of your consciousness, trying to attract your attention.

Questions to ask yourself – and what to do when the answer is 'yes'

Am I still haunted by feelings to do with something that happened some time in the past?

● You may be regretting a lost opportunity, grieving for a long-gone period of extreme happiness or plagued by memories of a traumatic event. Feelings like these can cripple your initiative and damage your relationships. Whether through spiritual healing, counselling or even hypnosis, it's essential to seek help in laying this ghost to rest. Only then will you be free to live fully in the present.

Am I secretly nurturing a fantasy?

● Cherishing a fantasy often implies a need to draw on more of your inner resources. You owe it to yourself to find ways of making your life more fulfilling. This could mean being more involved in relationships, considering a career change or expanding your range of skills.

Do I have a gift I need to develop?

● The first step is to find out what's holding you back. Is it laziness, a fear of failure or even a fear of success? Whatever its exact nature, I suggest you mentally lock it away. Tell yourself you can always retrieve it later, but life will be more fun if you leave it there whilst you find a way of developing your talent.

Old memories that haunt you may appear in dreams in the guise of a ghost.

Gipsy

Possible meanings

Dreaming about a gipsy often suggests a desire for freedom. If you have a mundane job, financial problems or feel trapped in a relationship, your dream could simply imply a wish to escape from your current concerns and responsibilities.

Your dream may though carry a more profound and hopeful message. The gipsy could represent a part of your own nature that places a high value on freedom of spirit. Your dream is not asking you to drop everything and take to the road, but it is encouraging you to take a fresh look at your lifestyle and ensure that it honours your spiritual, not just your material, values.

Questions to ask yourself – and what to do when the answer is 'yes'

Do you secretly long to abandon your inhibitions and release your 'inner gypsy'?

Do I feel trapped?
● It may be that you are constrained by responsibilities, perhaps family obligations, that you really cannot change. In this case, it's important to look after yourself as best you can. One way of doing this is to give yourself regular treats, however small. You would also benefit from making some changes in your daily routine.

Do I need to incorporate more of my spiritual values into my lifestyle?
● There are many ways of going about this, depending on your spiritual values. You may need to set aside regular time for meditation or prayer. It could also be good to simplify your life, clearing out unnecessary possessions or spending more time in nature. If you want to help others, many voluntary organizations would welcome your interest. The possibilities are endless.

Policeman

Possible meanings

Assuming that you are a law-abiding citizen, the policeman in your dream has a symbolic meaning. He is an inner authority figure who embodies the rules of conduct laid down by society and monitors your behaviour in this respect. Being chased by the police can therefore suggest that you feel guilty for harbouring unconventional tendencies. You may be afraid to act according to your own thoughts and feelings about what's right and try to fit in with others instead.

A policeman personifies the rules to which society expects us to adhere.

Your dream could also imply that, subconsciously, you feel you have committed a crime. Perhaps you feel you have let someone down by failing to live up to a standard they expect.

Recurring dreams about being in trouble with the police often mean that, deep down, you yearn to be a little less respectable.

Questions to ask yourself – and what to do when the answer is 'yes'

Am I reluctant to express my thoughts and feelings in case of the disapproval of others?

● Your dream suggests you are trying too hard to control your natural, healthy desire to be spontaneous. If you allow your need to conform to dominate your reactions, you will deprive yourself of one of life's great adventures – finding out who and what you are. It may be helpful to imagine that you are on your deathbed, reviewing your life. Will you be happy to say: 'I did my best to be conventional'?

Do I feel guilty about not living up to somebody's expectations?

● Please rest assured that you have an unnecessarily guilty conscience. Your real crime is your tendency to be too hard on yourself. The dream is encouraging you to learn to value your own individuality. You are here to make the best of yourself, not to be the person somebody else thinks you should be.

Do I feel I've become too respectable?

● Many people secretly feel like this, which perhaps explains why we often award celebrity status to people who behave outrageously or disobey the law. Your dream is not recommending that you to take to a life of crime. It is, though, encouraging you to be more a little more assertive and independent.

Journeys

Dreams about journeys almost always say something about your journey through life. Along the way you will inevitably encounter obstacles. Your dream can show you how to turn them into opportunities for personal development.

Setting off to an unknown destination implies entering a new phase in your waking life or taking a risk that will lead you into uncharted areas of emotional or spiritual experience. Are you enjoying the prospect of new adventures or feeling reluctant to enter foreign territory?

A dream about a difficult journey can reveal the way in which your own attitude is making your life hard going. It may imply, for instance, that you are overly passive and need to show more initiative. If you are willing to act on the insight the dream offers, you will start healing the negative attitudes that impede your progress.

Car

Possible meanings

A car is a vehicle that you take charge of and use to move yourself in a particular direction. In dreams it therefore represents the way in which you go through life, your motivation, ambition or drive.

Who is in the driving seat? If you are a passenger, the dream suggests that someone else is in charge of your life. Subconsciously, you are being driven by their expectations, values or prejudices. The dream could, alternatively, be warning you that you are being taken for a ride.

A damaged car or a faulty engine can signify illness, whilst running out of fuel reflects loss of energy. A car crash means that you have come to the end of a certain way of life.

If you lose control of the brakes or the steering, then your dream is alerting you to the fact that you are no longer in control of a situation in waking life. You may be driving yourself too hard or feeling helpless in the face of a problem.

Driving a more powerful car than you use in waking life suggests you are more ambitious than you realize. Dreams about losing your car can imply a loss of libido or drive. These often occur around mid-life and reflect a need to make changes in your lifestyle.

Questions to ask yourself – and what to do when the answer is 'yes'

Is somebody else making decisions for me?

● The dream is urging you to summon up the courage to take over the steering wheel of your own life. This means refusing to be dependent and asserting your right to do things in your own way instead. Otherwise you risk taking a back seat for the rest of your life.

Have I lost my motivation?

● You clearly need to find a new direction. This could mean a change of job, retraining for a new career or even considering a totally different way of life. You will find that as soon as you embark upon the new phase your energy will return.

Have I lost control of some area of my life?

● I suggest you start by reviewing your priorities. Have you taken on more responsibilities than you can handle? Are you making enough time for recreation and relaxation? If you don't pace yourself your health could suffer, so it's time to put your own well-being at the top of your agenda.

A car can represent the need to realize you are living life mechanically.

Bicycle

Dreaming you're in control of a bicycle reflects a balanced approach to life.

Possible meanings

Unlike most vehicles, a bicycle has no engine. To ride it you must use your own energy. Your dream is saying something about the need to travel through life in your own, individual way. Perhaps you are finding it hard to push the pedals round. This may mean that finding your own way of doing things seems too much like hard work. It could also imply that you're in a situation in which you feel you're getting nowhere.

A bicycle that is out of control implies a lack of balance somewhere in your life. An alternative meaning is that you are veering off course and need to refocus on your goal.

A pleasant dream in which you are happily pedalling along, enjoying the view, is a message that it's fine to carry on just as you are. In your waking life, you are heading in the right direction.

Questions to ask yourself – and what to do when the answer is 'yes'

Do I tend to go along with what others are doing?

● Do you ever wonder why you need to follow the crowd? Perhaps you were made to feel foolish for trying to do things differently when you were a child, and you still fear ridicule. Maybe you're afraid of making a mistake. But life will be far more stimulating when you start finding out what it feels like to do things your own way.

Do I feel as though I'm not getting anywhere?

● You may be underestimating yourself. Perhaps you are going more slowly than you'd like, but if you persevere you will eventually see results. On the other hand, if you are trying to do something for which you are temperamentally unsuited it would be wise to consider alternatives.

Do I need a better balance in some area of my life?

● You may be allowing your emotions or prejudices to get the better of you and would benefit from trying to cultivate a perspective that is wider and more compassionate.

Do I feel my life is out of control?

● Something has caused you to lose focus, and you need to make a sustained effort to get back on course. It would be good to enlist the help of someone whose strength of purpose you admire.

Train

Possible meanings

Trains convey large numbers of people along fixed tracks in the same direction. Once you're on a train you have only a limited number of pre-determined choices about where you can get on or off. A dream about a train journey can therefore suggest that you are moving through life in a passive, automatic way. A railway track represents rigid routines or inflexible attitudes and suggests the need for a more spontaneous approach.

Missing the train or being on the wrong train implies that you have lost an opportunity for social or professional advancement. If your dream features a derailed train, the message is that you have lost track of a goal you have been pursuing. Other meanings are also possible. Perhaps you have a tendency to lose track of your train of thought or to go 'off the rails' when you are under stress.

Perhaps you are at a station, desperately trying to find the correct platform. Since a station offers a choice of destinations, this dream suggests you have arrived at a point of transition in your waking life. You have the opportunity to take a new direction but you're not sure of which would be the best way to go.

Questions to ask yourself – and what to do when the answer is 'yes'

Do I have a passive approach to life?
● The less you think for yourself, the less meaningful your journey through life will become – and the harder it will be to change. Your dream is inviting you to practise choosing the options that suit you best as an individual.

Have I recently missed an opportunity to improve my circumstances?
● It may be that you were simply unprepared to deal with the situation and need to be more alert in future. However it's also worth asking yourself whether you have a subconscious resistance to change. If so, it's time to reflect on how much more interesting life would be if you made an effort to embrace new opportunities.

Am I unsure about which direction to go in next?
● I suggest you think carefully about your priorities. Do you want greater professional success, more friends or more money? Would you like the next phase to bring emotional or spiritual fulfilment? Once you have identified your aims, you will be in a position to make a wise choice.

Missing a train in a dream can be linked to a frustrating situation in your waking life.

Bus

Possible meanings

A bus carries many people along a prescribed route over which you have no choice. Dreaming about travelling by bus can therefore suggest that you are too inclined to fit in with what others are doing and need to become more enterprising.

Missing the bus can reflect a fear that you have failed to take advantage of an opportunity. Getting on the wrong bus indicates that you are involved in something that is not right for you.

If you failed to complete your education, or did badly at school, a dream about missing the school bus could be encouraging you to resume your studies, perhaps through adult education classes.

Questions to ask yourself – and what to do when the answer is 'yes'

Am I easily led?

● Your dream is urging you to take charge of your life. It may be that you are lazy and need to wake up to the fact that life is passing you by. If, though, you try to conform because you want others to approve of you, it's important to learn to stand up for your own way of doing things. You could benefit from a course of assertiveness training.

Am I worried about missing an opportunity?

● It's impossible to grasp every opportunity that comes your way, so I suggest you look at the situation from a more positive angle. One door may have closed, but another is bound to open in due course. Maybe, though, you let the opportunity pass you by because, subconsciously, you felt unable to cope with the consequences of taking it. In future it would be good to tell yourself that if you have the ability to rise to a challenge, then you also have the resources to deal with whatever happens as a result.

Am I getting involved in something that may be wrong for me?

● Your unconscious mind is trying to alert you to something you have not taken into account. It would be good to do a thorough review of the situation, with the particular aim of examining the motives of all concerned.

A dream of travelling on a bus can reveal how you feel about being in a group.

Plane

Possible meanings

Aeroplanes in dreams can have several symbolic meanings but they often imply a desire to travel a long way, very fast. Your dream may therefore indicate a yearning for higher status or a wish to pursue an ambitious goal.

If the plane takes off but never manages to gain height, the message may be that you are not fulfilling your potential. Although you have the ability to be a 'high-flier', you are holding yourself back and therefore cannot gain momentum. The dream could also indicate that you are finding it hard to get a new venture off the ground.

A plane crash sometimes indicates a loss of confidence in your ability to achieve a goal or fulfil an ambition. It can also suggest that your high hopes for a relationship or a project have come crashing down.

Waiting at an airport suggests that you are embarking on a new phase. If you are too late for your flight your dream is warning you against missing out on an opportunity that would bring you more freedom.

Taking off in a plane can signify a huge leap into the unknown.

Questions to ask yourself – and what to do when the answer is 'yes'

Am I working below my true capacity?

● You may be worried that people will be resentful or envious if you become more successful than them. Or maybe an insidious inner voice is whispering: 'Who do you think you are, anyway?'. One way of dealing with this is to write your own obituary. Would you want to be remembered for failing to fulfill your potential in case others disapproved?

Am I afraid I might not achieve my goal?

● Fear of failure can sometimes spur you on to greater efforts. However, if it's stopping you from trying to fulfil your aspirations, I urge you to take a deep breath and get on with it. Whether or not you succeed, making the effort to do so could bring opportunities you wouldn't otherwise have had.

Have my hopes or ideals come crashing down?

● Perhaps you were expecting too much. It's important, though, that you don't go to the opposite extreme and become cynical. Eventually, you will understand that your experience has taught you an invaluable lesson.

Flying

Possible meanings

You dream you are walking along when suddenly you find you are flying along above the ground, feeling blissfully happy. A dream like this often reflects a perfectly normal desire to enjoy the sensation of soaring free from the restrictions of worldly constraints. It could also mean, though, that you find the demands of daily life unbearably humdrum. You therefore try to escape by floating off into your own world.

If you are a natural 'high-flier', your dream may be urging you to give greater priority to fulfilling your inborn gifts. That exhilarating feeling in the dream is a taste of how your life could be more of the time. However, a dream in which you fly so high that you leave the earth far behind carries a warning about the dangers there are in being overambitious. It's also possible that your dream indicates a deep desire for spiritual experience.

A dream in which people are trying to pull you down to earth may mean that, in waking life, you are trying to escape the expectations that others have of you. If this isn't the case, the dream reflects an ongoing struggle you are having with a part of your own personality that wants you to lower your expectations. Could it be that, inwardly, you feel you don't deserve success?

Questions to ask yourself –
and what to do when the answer is 'yes'

Do I tend to live in a fantasy world?
● You clearly need to create a lifestyle that has more to offer. Energy you expend in daydreaming could be used for more creative ends.

Am I highly ambitious?
● Ambition can lead to great achievements, but if you let it rule your life it can create disaster. It would be as well to remind yourself of the story of Icarus, which you will find in the discussion about the 'Sun' (see page 75).

Do I yearn for spiritual experience?
● A spiritual search can take many forms. You may need to persevere with meditation or prayer, or look for a spiritual teacher. Maybe you would find the fulfilment you seek through creative work, or immersing yourself in an interest that makes your spirit soar. However, it would be good to bear in mind that moments of intense spiritual experience are the result of grace, not manipulation.

Do I secretly feel I don't deserve my success?

● You would be amazed to learn how many high achievers feel secretly unworthy. This is often the result of a cynical inner voice that says things like: 'People are bound to see through you eventually' or 'What's so special about you?'. It's essential that you close your mind to such poisonous suggestions.

**Dreams about flying often
compensate for feeling
weighed down in life.**

Boat

Being alone in a small boat can signify a sense of isolation or independence.

Possible meanings

Since water in dreams usually represents feelings, a boat could symbolize the way in which you are navigating the emotional side of life. If others are with you on the boat, the dream may reflect a 'relationship' issue.

Crossing an ocean suggests that you are undertaking a voyage of discovery. Maybe you are embarking on a new career or a different lifestyle. If the boat is becalmed though, the dream suggests that your life is currently at a standstill or, alternatively, that you are 'all at sea' and don't know which direction to take.

A smooth trip in a sailing boat implies that something you thought would be tricky is proving to be 'plain sailing'. Whereas missing a boat indicates that you have lost an opportunity as a result of bad timing. A sinking boat represents the end of a relationship, or the failure of a project.

Questions to ask yourself – and what to do when the answer is 'yes'

Am I having problems with a group of people?
● Since you are all in the same boat, it's important to be tolerant. With ongoing dialogue and goodwill on the part of all, issues can be resolved.

Do I feel I am not making any progress?
● If your best efforts to move forward have not succeeded, and you genuinely feel that nothing else you can say or do would make a difference, then your dream is urging you to change direction.

Am I feeling all at sea?
● You need to find somebody who has a 'compass'. Perhaps a career counsellor would fit the bill, by helping you to assess your skills and experience. Alternatively, you may benefit from asking a therapist to help you explore your current lack of orientation.

Do I feel I've missed the boat?
● You may be kicking yourself for being too slow on the uptake, but please do your best to see this episode as a lesson not a tragedy. Other opportunities will come your way if you remain alert to possibilities.

Does some aspect of my life seem to be coming to an end?
● Sometimes you have no choice but to give up on a situation. It would be better to find a more promising outlet for your energy.

Crossing a bridge

Possible meanings

Since a bridge joins up two distinctly different locations, dreams about crossing a bridge often indicate that you are in the process of leaving behind one phase of your life and moving forward into a new situation.

If the bridge is unsafe, you may be concerned about how current changes will affect your security. However, the dream could also be warning you that your aims are unrealistic.

Perhaps you are stuck on the bridge. This usually means that, although you are trying to make changes in your life, you are finding it hard to let go of the past and move on.

A bridge can also represent a connection with another person. Maybe you are trying to get closer to someone or are attempting a reconciliation after a period of estrangement.

**Questions to ask yourself –
and what to do when the answer is 'yes'**

Am I worried in case a current change in my circumstances threatens my security?

● I think it's true to say that most people feel apprehensive in the face of radical change. Whether you are leaving your job, ending a relationship, moving house or finishing college, you may find it comforting to tell yourself that fear of the unknown is a normal reaction. What's important is to avoid letting your insecurities overwhelm you. If, though, you are on the verge of undertaking something unwise, your sense of foreboding could be a warning about the need to reassess your plans.

Do I need to let go and move on?

● If you feel stuck, you would find it helpful to identify what it is that's holding you back. Is there something you feel you've left unfinished? Are you worried in case what lies ahead is no improvement on your previous situation? I suggest you focus on the exciting new opportunities that the next phase is bound to bring.

Am I hoping to get closer to someone?

● If you feel genuine love and respect for this person, you don't need to worry about finding the right words or doing the right thing. You need only express your feelings as best you can. Lead from the heart and you will go a long way towards bridging the gap between you.

A bridge can represent the process of transition to a new stage of life.

Outdoors

Feeling free to be the person nature intended you to be is the basis of psychological health. Dreams about nature therefore carry an especially healing message.

The landscape in your dream reflects your emotional state. Notice whether you feel comfortable there or ill at ease. Is there a situation in your waking life that arouses similar feelings? A place that's unfamiliar symbolizes an area of your inner world that you need to explore. Is it easy to move through, or full of obstacles? Do you feel curious or fearful?

Nature offers a wealth of metaphors on which your dream can seize. You may need to resolve a stormy situation, learn to go with the flow, or admit that everything in the garden is not as lovely as it seems. This section will help you to understand the symbolic significance of different natural settings.

River

Possible meanings

A river is like life – just as the water is forever moving on, so too is life. A dream about being immersed in a river therefore implies that you are caught up in a process of natural change beyond your control. All you can do is relax and surrender to it.

If you are standing on the bank of the river, watching it flow past, your dream could be warning you against allowing life to pass you by. Perhaps you are failing to seize an opportunity or trying to play safe by looking at life as though you are a detached observer.

Since rivers often mark boundaries, crossing a river signifies moving into a different state of consciousness. Your dream suggests that you are ready to adopt a new outlook, or maybe even a different lifestyle.

Questions to ask yourself – and what to do when the answer is 'yes'

Am I struggling against the current rather than going with the flow?
● Your dream is challenging you to trust the process of life. If you are someone who always likes to be in control, you need to learn that trying to manipulate a situation or a person can actually stop your destiny unfolding in the best possible way. It's far more exhilarating to allow the tide of events to carry you forward, even if at first it feels a little scary.

Do I tend to be too passive?
● The eminent psychologist Carl Jung warned against living what he called the 'provisional life', or standing on the sidelines instead of actively participating. You owe it to yourself to start enjoying the great adventure of finding out who you are and what you are capable of.

Have I reached a point of transition?
● Your dream confirms that you are ready to experience life in a totally new way, so you need not hesitate to embrace change wholeheartedly.

The ceaseless flow of a river is a metaphor for the ever-moving passage of time.

Mountain

Possible meanings

You are physically closer to the heavens on top of a mountain than anywhere else on earth, so mountains traditionally signify spiritual aspirations. They also represent the quest for self-knowledge. Climbing a mountain can therefore indicate a need to develop your spiritual side or to become more self-aware.

Your dream may also reflect the fact that you are taking steps to achieve a goal. This can sometimes be uphill work. If you are faced with apparently insurmountable obstacles you could be pursuing the wrong goal, or trying to climb too high for your own good.

A dream of standing on top of a mountain sometimes suggests that you have reached the peak of your success or the height of your ambitions. However, if you aren't sure about the direction that your life is taking, the mountain dream is encouraging you to take an overview of your circumstances.

Questions to ask yourself –
and what to do when the answer is 'yes'

Do I need to focus on my spiritual growth?
● Spirituality means different things to different people. If you are drawn to an established religious path, it would be good to explore more of what it has to offer. You may want to learn meditation or simply spend time in places you find inspiring. Perhaps you'd like to explore your inner world with the help of a therapist or spiritual counsellor. There's no right or wrong way. All that matters is that you follow the path to which you feel most drawn.

Am I finding it hard to achieve a goal?
● You could be aiming too high. There's no shame in knowing your limitations and you may be more successful if you set your sights elsewhere. Otherwise, try to treat the obstacles you meet as opportunities to draw on your inner resources and find a different way of reaching your goal.

Have I achieved my ambition?
● The dream is a message that you can't go any higher, so it's pointless to push yourself to do even more – and could even be harmful. You can now afford to relax and enjoy the fruits of your hard work.

Do I need to review the direction my life is taking?

● I suggest you look at your current situation as a drama. Do you like the role you are playing? If not, how would you change it? What would you like to see happening in the next act?

From the top of a mountain you can see the bigger picture.

Volcano

A volcano that is erupting can signify an outburst of rage

Possible meanings

The precise meaning of your dream depends on whether or not the volcano is active. If it's dormant, you may be suppressing fiery emotions like sexual passion, anger or revenge. Alternatively, a volcano spewing out fire represents feelings so powerful that they could erupt at any time and create havoc.

Since fire can also represent creative energy, an active volcano sometimes symbolizes a breakthrough in your awareness of how to approach a challenging task or situation.

Questions to ask yourself – and what to do when the answer is 'yes'

Am I repressing feelings to which I'd rather not admit?

● From time to time, we all have feelings that don't conform to the image we have of ourselves. You may think it's wrong to feel like this but it's important to accept that, like all of us, you have a dark side. It's part of human nature. You don't have to act on your feelings and it could even be dangerous to do so. But you do need to acknowledge them. Otherwise they may boil over and cause damage.

Do I feel so frustrated that I'm ready to explode?

● Before things can improve, you need to understand why you are so reluctant to express those pent-up emotions. You may find that drawing, painting or writing about the situation will help to identify whatever it is that's holding you back. Then you'll be free to confront the issue constructively.

Am I faced with a challenge with which I feel unable to deal?

● I highly recommend that you stop thinking of the situation as a problem. Instead, try to see it as an opportunity to create something more positive and rewarding. Moving beyond your comfort zone may not be easy but will, in the end, help you to feel more alive.

Ocean

Possible meanings

Since life originated in water, the ocean often symbolizes the source of life. Your dream may therefore tell you something about the feminine side of your nature. It could also be commenting on your relationship with your mother.

The ocean can also represent the realm of the unconscious mind. In this case, the dream is encouraging you to get in touch with your inner world. It may be that you are afraid of discovering something hideous lurking within its depths, like a monster in a myth or a movie.

Oceans are also a metaphor for the source of our inspiration and creative potential. A dream about swimming in the ocean may suggest a need to immerse yourself in a creative process. If you have an overwhelming sense of being at one with everything as you swim, your dream could also relate to powerful sexual feelings. Alternatively, it may reflect the extent to which you are 'in the swim', or able to express and act on your feelings.

Questions to ask yourself – and what to do when the answer is 'yes'

Am I troubled by relationship issues, perhaps with my mother?

● Your first experience of feminine nature was through your mother. If yours was an unhappy experience, you may have sustained emotional wounds that need healing before you can enjoy fulfilling relationships with others. Your dream is therefore inviting you to focus on your sensitive, intuitive side and it may be worth you finding a therapist to help you with this complex issue.

Am I afraid that, deep down, I am a nasty person?

● You may be comforted to know that this is a very common fear. Most of us, unless we are saintly, have thoughts and feelings we wouldn't care to reveal to others. Condemning yourself for having a darker side will serve only to undermine your self-confidence. If, though, you are tempted to act out your more destructive impulses, then you are right to be concerned and should seek professional help immediately.

Am I feeling unusually creative or sexually aware?

● Your dream suggests that a wealth of hidden potential is now available to you, so you need only go with the flow and draw on it. As your sexuality blossoms, a relationship could take on a new lease of life.

Swimming in the ocean suggests feeling deeply at one with nature.

Earthquake

Possible meanings

An earthquake often implies a serious emotional upheaval. Something in your life, perhaps a relationship, a job or a project in which you've been involved, has unexpectedly fallen apart, leaving you feeling that you are no longer on solid ground. It's also possible that you are faced with the need for major change, something of which the mere thought makes you quake with fear.

You can also dream of an earthquake if you have based an important decision on an assumption you have discovered was totally mistaken.

Sometimes, an earthquake can relate to unexpressed emotions that have been rumbling around in the depths of your psyche but can no longer be suppressed.

Questions to ask yourself – and what to do when the answer is 'yes'

Am I reeling with shock from an emotional trauma?
● Once the shock has died down, you will need to face the challenge of adapting to the new circumstances. Your emotional wounds will start healing once you can stop focusing on what you have lost and start drawing on your inner resources to create something new. This can sometimes be easier to do with the appropriate professional help.

Am I afraid of drastic change that cannot be avoided?
● Few people welcome change that disrupts their current circumstances. Yet the sooner you can accept it, the easier it will be to handle the consequences. Perhaps you have automatically assumed that the new situation will leave you worse off in some way. One way of counteracting these fears is to imagine, as vividly as possible, how much more stimulating and fulfilling your life will be once the change has actually happened.

Has something I believed was true proved otherwise?
● Perhaps you have been a little too eager to believe what you wanted to believe. Your dream is alerting you to the important need to cultivate a more objective attitude, so that in future you can take better care of your own interests.

Earthquakes can symbolize the dire consequences of unleashing suppressed feelings.

Tidal wave or flooding

Possible meanings

You're on a beach when you suddenly see an enormous tidal wave surging towards the shore. You take shelter in a nearby building but the giant waves come crashing against the walls. You realize that it's only a matter of time before you drown.

A tidal wave is a powerful natural force. Nothing and nobody can stop it. As a dream symbol it sometimes represents an unavoidable process that arouses overwhelming feelings of fear. Your dream could therefore indicate that you are faced with inexorable, but unwelcome, change.

Since water usually symbolizes emotions, huge waves can also represent powerful feelings welling up from deep within you, threatening to break through your defences. Your dream is a warning that you have less control over a situation than you think. If you long to change an unfulfilling lifestyle but are worried about upsetting others, the dream could indicate a subconscious desire to 'make waves'.

If the tidal wave looms up yet causes no harm, you need not be anxious about allowing your feelings to surface. They may cause an upheaval, but not the devastation you fear. Flood waters are not only destructive. They also fertilize territory that would otherwise remain dry and arid.

A tidal wave warns of the danger of being overwhelmed by emotion.

Questions to ask yourself – and what to do when the answer is 'yes'

Am I afraid of change I can see looming on the horizon?
● If you do your best to welcome change, you will find the new situation more stimulating, and ultimately more enjoyable, than you had anticipated. Since you have no option, you may as well take the plunge.

Am I trying to suppress some powerful emotions?
● Your dream suggests that you cannot protect yourself from the full impact of an intense emotional experience. What matters here is how you deal with it. If you maintain your self-control, you will make some very big, dangerous waves. Are you prepared to take responsibility for the consequences?

Am I torn between seeking greater fulfilment and upsetting others?
● It looks as though you are inundated with too many conflicting demands and urgently need to create a better balance. Your dream is urging you to find ways of meeting more of your own needs, even if this means being less available for others.

Storm

Possible meanings

A dream about being caught in a storm often suggests that you are involved in a stormy relationship or work situation. It can also indicate that a conflict is raging within you, making you prone to uncontrolled outbursts of violent emotion. On the other hand it could simply mean you have a deep desire to take the world by storm!

Thunder represents rumblings of anger, whilst lightning may signify a flash of inspiration, a sudden awareness of the need for major change, or a blinding revelation you cannot ignore.

Questions to ask yourself – and what to do when the answer is 'yes'

Am I involved in a stormy relationship?
● Most conflicts are the result of lack of communication between those concerned, so an aggressive attitude will do nothing to heal the situation. It would be much better to ask yourself what you really want from the other person, and to try and understand what he or she wants from you. You may not agree with their point of view, but it's important to respect their feelings and, if you can, meet them halfway.

Is a stormy situation raging at work?
● It may be best to resolve matters by involving someone you can trust to act as a mediator and help you negotiate. If you are to weather the storm successfully, everyone concerned needs to feel that they have won something.

Am I prone to violent emotional outbursts?
● Your dream is a message about the need to come to terms with your turbulent feelings. It's time to let go of old resentments or unfulfilled expectations and realize where your true priorities lie. You may find it helpful to imagine that you are very old and looking back on your life. As you review the current situation, what advice would you give yourself?

Do I long to take the world by storm?
● You need to think the unthinkable, be bold – and above all, to step outside your comfort zone and try new ways of doing things. If you can dream it, you can do it!

Although a storm may be terrifying, it will clear the air.

Ice

Possible meanings

Since water generally symbolizes emotions, ice can symbolize a cold, unapproachable side of your nature. Perhaps your feelings have been in cold storage as the result of a trauma. Maybe you are seen as insensitive when you are petrified.

Skating on thin ice can expose you to dangers that are hidden.

If a relationship has reached stalemate or you feel as though you've been left out in the cold, the dream may be encouraging you to break the ice. It could also carry a warning that you are involved in a potentially destructive situation, as if you were skating on thin ice.

Sometimes the ice has a more positive significance. If you are inclined to be too sentimental, for instance, you may benefit from taking a cold, objective look at something.

Questions to ask yourself – and what to do when the answer is 'yes'

Do I keep others at an emotional distance?

● Your life could be so much more fulfilling. I highly recommend you seek professional help to face the underlying problem and heal your fear of involvement.

Do I need to effect a reconciliation?

● Admitting your own part in creating the rupture may cost you a little pride but could pay handsome dividends. Sometimes you simply have to make allowances for other people's shortcomings, as well as your own human frailty.

Am I involved in a situation that could be harmful?

● I wonder what is stopping you from detaching yourself. Could it be that you secretly get a kick from flirting with danger? Please be aware that it's fine to do whatever you want to – as long as you're prepared to take responsibility for the consequences.

Do I need to be more objective?

● The dream is urging you to err on the side of ruthlessness, especially if you are usually a little too soft and easily influenced.

Desert

Possible meanings

The meaning of your dream depends on your feelings about being in the desert. Perhaps you have a sense of joyful anticipation as you look into the far distance and see unlimited possibilities, with nothing to block your vision. On the other hand, your dream could signify profound loneliness or an emotionally barren existence. It could also reflect feelings of desolation because somebody has deserted you.

Since there are few manmade structures in deserts, they were traditionally thought of as pure environments in which you might receive divine revelation. It's possible then that your dream indicates a desire for some sort of spiritual experience.

Questions to ask yourself – and what to do when the answer is 'yes'

Do my horizons seem to be expanding?

● Now is the time to pursue your dreams, explore your potential or make decisions you've been putting off. Your expansive feelings are unlikely to last indefinitely so it's important to take the initiative and get in touch with people who could help you.

Do I feel isolated and empty?

● Your dream is an urgent message that you need to seek help. I recommend that you start by seeing your doctor to find out if you need treatment for depression. Depending on the outcome, you may then want to consider having therapy or, if it feels more appropriate, seeking spiritual counselling.

Do I have a yearning for deep spiritual experience?

● It would be good to take a little time out, perhaps at a retreat, where there is nothing to distract you from an intense experience of your inner world. Bearing in mind the saying that 'when the pupil is ready, the teacher will come', be aware that somebody you meet now could be your spiritual teacher, even though they may not advertise themselves as such.

Shifting sands may be a metaphor for feeling unsure of your position.

Forest

Possible meanings

Since trees are a traditional symbol for life force, a forest usually symbolizes your innermost nature. A dream in which you are walking in a forest can therefore indicate a need to get in touch with your deepest feelings about a person or situation. Being lost in a forest suggests that you are feeling overwhelmed, unable to see the wood for the trees.

A forest can signify a need for deeper understanding of your own nature.

Questions to ask yourself – and what to do when the answer is 'yes'

Am I unsure of my real feelings about someone or something?

● It could be that the incessant chatter of your mind, as it weighs up the pros and cons of the situation, is preventing you from hearing the voice of your heart. One effective way of calming a busy mind is to spend some time alone, in a natural setting. You don't literally have to go to a forest, but communing with nature in some form will allow your feelings to emerge.

Do I feel overwhelmed by events?

● You may be trying too hard to meet too many demands on your time and attention. It's time to step back and decide where your main priorities lie. You may find it helpful to discuss your predicament with someone whose judgment you value. I also recommend that you start disentangling yourself from people and situations that sap your energy.

Garden

Possible meanings

Dreams about gardens are usually encouraging you to enhance your well-being by cultivating an aspect of your personality or improving your circumstances. The specific meaning depends on what you are doing in the garden. Digging, for instance, suggests preparing the ground for something you have in mind, whilst planting implies a desire to put down roots.

A well-kept, flourishing garden can reflect a period of growth in your personal development.

If the garden is neglected, you may need to weed out negative attitudes or bad habits, sort out your priorities or organize an area of your life where chaos rules.

Flowers suggest
flourishing relationships
and sensual pleasures.

Questions to ask yourself –
and what to do when the answer is 'yes'

Do I need to make more of myself?
● Whatever you are doing in the dream is the symbolic key to the next step. Perhaps you need to dig out information, or sow the seeds of a new project by talking to people who are in a position to help you establish something.

Is everything in my life currently going well?
● Your upbeat mood means that this is a good time to stretch yourself by exploring new possibilities.

Is there an area of my life that badly needs sorting out?
● This may mean something as simple as clearing out clutter. It's also possible that you need to tackle a bad habit, in which case you could benefit from listening to a self-hypnosis recording that addresses this issue. If you've been neglecting a relationship, the dream is urging you to make more effort to communicate.

Cliff

A cliff can reflect anxiety about maintaining your foothold on a situation.

Possible meanings

A dream of falling off a cliff is alerting you to a potentially dangerous situation. Perhaps you're being overambitious or taking the moral high ground with no real justification.

Maybe you don't actually fall, but just manage to hang on to the edge of the cliff. In this case, the dream is warning you that you've reached the limit of your physical, emotional or financial resources.

Jumping or being pushed off a cliff often indicates a pressing need to come down to earth. If this doesn't apply to you, then your dream could be urging you to take a leap into the unknown.

Questions to ask yourself – and what to do when the answer is 'yes'

Am I aiming too high?

● Your dream is warning you against pushing your luck. There's nothing wrong with being ambitious, but both you and those around you could suffer if you lose sight of reality. You would be wise to avoid acting on impulse.

Am I currently taking the moral high ground?

● Your dream is a message that you are in danger of appearing sanctimonious and need to cultivate humility. Otherwise people will be tempted to try and cut you down to size.

Am I feeling overwhelmed by circumstances?

● It looks as though you are trying to fulfil too many demands on your time and energy. In order to protect your own interests, I suggest that you refuse to accept further responsibilities and cut down on existing obligations wherever possible. Unless you feel free to say 'no' saying 'yes' is just a habit, not a meaningful choice.

Am I being a little too idealistic?

● It's fine to have your head in the clouds, as long as you keep your feet planted firmly on the ground. You need to tailor your expectations to what is feasible in practice.

Cave

Possible meanings

Caves were traditionally thought of as the womb of the earth goddess and were often used as the setting for secret initiation ceremonies during which participants would undergo a symbolic death and rebirth. Dreams about caves can therefore occur when you are undergoing a rite of passage, such as the onset of middle age, when aspects of your personality that you've outgrown need to die.

A cave can also symbolize a situation pregnant with possibilities. Deep inside, you may be incubating a new attitude that will radically change your relationship to someone or something. The dream could also indicate that you are looking forward to a new lease of life or considering a change of lifestyle. Less positively, it may reflect a feeling that you have 'caved in' to somebody rather than standing your ground.

Questions to ask yourself –
and what to do when the answer is 'yes'

Am I embarking on a new phase?
● Your dream is inviting you to reassess your priorities. The more willing you are to embrace change, the more invigorating and meaningful the next stage of your life will be.

Are my feelings about someone or something changing?
● A gradual process of transformation has begun deep within your psyche. Old hurts may be healing, expectations changing or new insights emerging that will in due course radically change a relationship or situation. All you need do is be patient.

Am I hoping to alter my lifestyle?
● Your dream suggests that, subconsciously, you are preparing for major change, but you're not yet ready to take practical steps.

Dreaming about a cave may imply a need to reflect inwardly on your motives.

Moon

The moon signifies a need to be guided by your intuition.

Possible meanings

The moon is traditionally associated with romance, inspiration, madness and mystery, so may feature in a dream if you have fallen madly in love, have a romantic outlook or feel inspired by somebody.

With its constantly changing cycles, the moon has been a traditional symbol of feminine consciousness in nearly all cultures. Your dream could therefore be encouraging you to get in touch with the wisdom of your feminine nature.

A new moon suggests the start of something new in your life or, sometimes, a feeling of being spiritually reborn. If the moon is full, the dream implies that a situation has developed as far as it can. For people in their middle years, it can signify the end of an era and the need to prepare for the second half of life.

A waxing moon implies a period of creative growth, or developments in your personality, and often features in the dreams of pregnant women. A waning moon may be a metaphor for a dwindling interest in something or somebody. It could, alternatively, indicate a need to pay more attention to the promptings of your intuition.

Questions to ask yourself –
and what to do when the answer is 'yes'

Do I have a romantic view of someone or something?
● Although you may be basking in the warmth of a romantic glow, your dream could be a gentle reminder not to lose sight of reality.

Do I need to get in touch with my feminine side?
● If you're more at home with reason and logic, you may tend to dismiss your feelings or intuitive hunches as irrational. Yet they are the voice of your wise feminine nature, offering you a different, yet invaluable perspective. Feminine consciousness sheds a soft, forgiving light, revealing that which is often hidden from the bright light of reason.

Am I in my middle years?
● Until now, you have probably directed your energy outwards into your work and your domestic situation. Around mid-life, though, it's psychologically healthy to place more emphasis on your inner life. Now is the time to reassess your values, and to cultivate serenity by making time for reflection and meditation.

Sun

Possible meanings

The sun can symbolize vitality, clarity, creative power and the light of intelligence. In some dreams it is associated with masculine authority or heroic deeds. If the sun is uncomfortably hot, the dream could be warning you against being overly intellectual.

As a symbol of divine power the sun represents your own inner light. In this case, your dream suggests a need to be more aware of your spiritual side.

A dream about the sunrise can indicate the beginning of a new phase in your life or the start of a relationship. It may also suggest renewed energy, determination or insight. If your dream takes place at sunset, it reflects the end of a cycle, a relationship that's no longer viable, or a decline in your energy.

Questions to ask yourself –
and what to do when the answer is 'yes'

Would I like to achieve something heroic?
● Ambition is a fine thing, as long as you don't aim so high that you lose touch with reality. It would be as well to remember the old cautionary tale of Icarus. Using wings made of wax, he flew too near the sun – with predictably disastrous results. If you are a woman, your dream may be warning you against allowing your goal-oriented masculine side to overwhelm your receptive, feminine energy and harm your relationships.

Do I tend to be overanalytical?
● You may have an underlying fear of being spontaneous, perhaps as a result of feeling threatened or humiliated when you were a child. That small person still exists somewhere within your psyche, subtly influencing your responses to people and situations. I suggest you hold an imaginary dialogue with this younger version of yourself, so that it feels valued not victimized.

Do I need to explore my spiritual side?
● If conventional religion does not meet your needs, there are plenty of alternatives on offer – but please be discriminating. You can find innumerable workshops and gurus out there, but many offer only a kind of pseudo-spirituality, for which there is often a considerable charge. Trust your instincts to guide you towards the right path for you.

A dream featuring the sun could help you to shed light on a situation.

Buildings

A building represents the basic structure of your psyche, the belief systems you have constructed during the course of your life that determine your attitudes and your behaviour. This means that dreams featuring buildings often indicate a need to challenge your assumptions about a person or a situation. Adopting a more balanced perspective will make you feel more alive and may also help to heal a rift in a relationship.

As you will see in this section, different buildings relate to different areas of your life. Notice how you feel about the building. Being trapped in it suggests that your viewpoint is too narrow and you need to cultivate a more open-minded approach. If you are exploring the building, the dream implies you are ready to embrace new possibilities.

Workplace

Possible meanings

A dream set in your workplace can reflect your feelings about your job, or concerns about how well you're performing. You may feel ambivalent about taking on additional responsibilities or taking a more proactive role.

If the dream features your relationship with your boss, it may be inviting you to focus on finding a way of resolving current difficulties. It's also possible, though, that your dream is using the image of your boss to reveal underlying issues you have with authority.

It's not uncommon to dream you work in a factory, even though, in reality, you may never have set foot in one. Since factories are places where goods of a uniform standard are manufactured to order, this dream carries a warning that you are in danger of losing your individuality.

Questions to ask yourself – and what to do when the answer is 'yes'

Am I worried about my performance at work?
● Your dream could reflect either your general concerns or a specific source of anxiety such as a forthcoming appraisal. You will put yourself in a stronger position if you are prepared to acknowledge the areas in which you are weak. It could be good to take the initiative and ask for suggestions as to how you might improve.

Am I involved in a power struggle with my boss?
● Since you cannot win this battle, I recommend that you find a way of making the relationship work to your advantage. Your role is to support your boss. How can you do this more effectively? If you have a history of antagonizing those in positions of power, you could have underlying problems relating to your own sense of authority. Your dream is a message about the need to resolve them, if necessary with professional help.

Do I feel like a cog in a machine?
● Your dream is alerting you to your tendency to conform to other people's expectations. If you apply your own standards to the choices you make you will soon regain your sense of integrity.

A dream about a problem you have at work may offer you the solution.

High building

Possible meanings

You are stuck at the top of a high building. You hate being so high up and are desperate to have your feet on firm ground. Or maybe you're standing on a roof, terrified of falling but paralyzed with fear.

Being in a high place often suggests a tendency to live in your head. Your dream could also imply, though, that you feel you are in some way superior to others.

A dream about being trapped in a high place can reflect a sense of being isolated from everything that makes you feel secure. You can have this dream if you have moved to another area, far from the safety of your old, familiar environment.

Being in a high building could imply that you are out of touch with reality.

Questions to ask yourself –
and what to do when the answer is 'yes'

Am I inclined to live in my head?

● Your dream is encouraging you to put more effort into your relation-ships. If you tend to be a loner, you could consider joining a group of people who have similar interests or taking a class in a subject you'd like to explore. That way, you would satisfy both your intellect and your need for contact with others.

Do I secretly feel I'm somehow better than other people?

● Whatever the reason for your lofty stance, it's important to bear in mind that pride comes before a fall. If you are trying to make an impres-sion, a warmer, more human approach will produce better results.

Am I feeling isolated?

● It's important that you don't allow your insecurities to get the better of you. I recommend that you find a way of contributing to your local community, especially If you have moved to an area where you know nobody. Perhaps you have skills that a voluntary organization would welcome. Or maybe you'd like to explore the possibility of visiting an elderly person who lives alone, or helping out in a local hospital.

Hospital

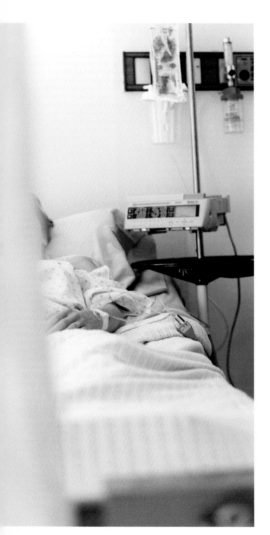

A hospital implies healing but can suggest you feel at the mercy of circumstances.

Possible meanings

If you are worried about your health or are about to go into hospital, then your dream may simply reflect your current feelings of anxiety. Often, though, a dream that is set in a hospital implies that you are undergoing a process of emotional or spiritual healing.

Other meanings are also possible. If you are feeling tired and vulnerable, your dream could indicate a longing to be looked after. However, it could also suggest a deep desire to give up responsibility for your own well-being.

A dream about being in hospital even though you are perfectly healthy suggests a conflict within your personality. An inner, critical voice is trying to persuade you that something is wrong with your attitudes or your beliefs.

Questions to ask yourself – and what to do when the answer is 'yes'

Am I worried about my health?
● It's important to put your mind at rest, so please see your doctor. Your fears may prove groundless but, if not, it would be best to have treatment sooner rather than later.

Am I feeling emotionally vulnerable?
● If you are under a lot of stress, you need to ensure you get enough rest and relaxation. At times like this it's good to turn to friends for support, and to nurture yourself emotionally. This could mean walking in the country, listening to music, gardening, or doing anything else that satisfies your soul.

Am I tired of being responsible for my own well-being?
● On a bad day, freedom of choice can seem less like a privilege to be cherished than a burden to be borne. Your dream is alerting you to the importance of making choices that enrich your life.

Am I worried in case my beliefs are wrong?
● Your dream is encouraging you to trust your intuition and assert your right to go your own way. It's better to make a mistake and retain your integrity than to conform without question.

Hotel

Possible meanings

Hotels can have different symbolic meanings but they sometimes imply a desire to escape from your home circumstances. More often, though, a hotel represents a temporary phase or situation. Take notice of whether it's run-down, uncomfortable, and in need of renovation, or enjoyable and relaxing.

If you have misgivings about a relationship, the dream could confirm your fears that it will not last. On a more optimistic note, it may mean that the relationship is in a period of transition and will ultimately improve.

Since a hotel is a place where you live alongside strangers who are constantly coming and going, your dream could also reflect a need for more privacy in your waking life.

Questions to ask yourself – and what to do when the answer is 'yes'

Would I like to escape from my domestic situation?

● I suggest you think of yourself as being in transition. You therefore need to be patient. Life may be difficult at present but when, in due course, you look back at this phase, you will realize that it was the necessary prelude to a new – and better – situation.

Am I in a relationship I suspect may not last?

● If you are enjoying the relationship and want it to carry on for the time being, it's important to be ruthlessly honest with yourself. Are you genuinely happy to live for the day, without expecting anything more permanent? If so, that's fine. Maybe, though, you secretly hope for something more. Unless you have good reason to believe that this could happen, you'd be wise to consider ending the relationship to avoid emotional damage.

Do I need more privacy?

● It's important to find a way of making more space for yourself. Perhaps you need to learn to say 'no' more often, and take time out to meditate, go for a walk, or do whatever helps to recharge your batteries. Is there a room in your home that you could claim as your own, so that when you feel hemmed in you have a place to which you can retreat?

A hotel can represent a sense of impermanence in a current situation.

Department store

Possible meanings

A department store offers a huge range of goods for sale. Your dream could, then, relate to a situation in which you need to choose from a number of available options or opportunities. If, deep down, you know exactly what you want, the dream is encouraging you to follow your instincts. But if you are feeling overwhelmed by the choices on offer, the message is that you need to be more decisive.

Perhaps you want to buy something but have reservations about the price. This may reflect a fear that the ulitmate cost of seizing an opportunity could be too high, but it could also imply that you don't value yourself enough.

A dream about window-shopping can simply suggest a desire for things you can't really afford. However it sometimes means that you enjoy fantasizing about having what you want but can't be bothered to exert yourself in order to get it.

Shopping in a department store implies a need to be discriminating.

Questions to ask yourself – and what to do when the answer is 'yes'

Do I need to be more decisive?
● Sometimes it's better to do something, or even to make an arbitrary choice, than to agonize endlessly over your decision and eventually end up doing nothing. Even an apparently 'wrong' choice can ultimately turn out to be right.

Am I worried about the implications of taking an opportunity?
● If you know, deep down, that accepting an offer will be so demanding that your health or your relationships will suffer, then you would clearly be wise to refuse it. First, though, you may want to try and negotiate more congenial terms. However, if your anxiety is based on a feeling that you don't really deserve this opportunity, I recommend that you 'feel the fear and do it anyway'. Rising to the challenge will help you to overcome your self-doubt.

Do I want things that are beyond my means?
● If you ask yourself what it is you really want, I suspect you will find the answer is a stronger sense of your own worth. You could begin by taking stock of your life, making a list of everything you feel is positive about yourself and your life. If you find it hard to be objective, why not ask a friend to help you?

Cinema

Possible meanings

To visit a cinema is to enter a world of illusions. Your dream may therefore reflect a tendency to live in a fantasy world. But even if you are firmly grounded in reality, the dream could be urging you to question your assumptions about a situation or a relationship. The message is that something is not as you believe it to be.

Another meaning is also possible. Since a cinema is a place where images are projected your dream may be inviting you to focus on how you put yourself across to others. On the whole, people will take you at face value. This means that if you don't present yourself in the way you'd like to be seen, you won't get the response for which you hope.

Is a situation what it seems – or are you mistaking illusion for reality?

Questions to ask yourself – and what to do when the answer is 'yes'

Do I tend to live in a fantasy world?

● Perhaps you don't find your daily routine stimulating. Your dream is urging you to wake up and realize that it's up to you to make your life more interesting. While it's fine to exercise your imagination, you also need to draw on your resources and start turning some of those daydreams into reality.

Am I taking someone or something for granted?

● Unless you are in the habit of questioning your assumptions, it's all too easy to become complacent. Your dream is encouraging you to look at a person or a situation with a fresh eye. You could start by paying particular attention to niggling doubts or slight feelings of unease. They may be warning you against mistaking appearances for reality.

Do I need to consider how I put myself across to others?

● If people tend to take advantage of you, or if things never work out as you'd like them to, you may be giving off the wrong signals. Maybe you appear eager to please or easy-going when that's not how you feel. Your dream is encouraging you to create an image that's more representative of the real you. To start with, you may find it helpful to think of someone whose attitude you admire and use them as a role model.

House and home

A house in a dream represents your self whilst the rooms symbolize different aspects of your personality. Just as a house has different floors, your psyche has many levels. The further down you go, the closer you are to the realm of the unconscious, which is often represented by a cellar. The lower floors relate to your social and interpersonal skills, whilst the topmost storey signifies your spiritual and intellectual aspirations. A dream that features the façade of a house says something about the face you tend to show the world. An old house can imply old-fashioned attitudes or a yearning for the past.

Your dream may be encouraging you to put your inner house in order by coming to terms with hurtful memories or cleaning out negative attitudes. This deeply healing process will set you free to become the person you are meant to be.

House

Possible meanings

Since a house symbolizes your self, your dream says something about your current physical or emotional state.

A dilapidated house may reflect a physical injury or a health challenge. Your dream could also be a wake-up call to repair the damage incurred by harbouring negative attitudes or neglecting deep needs. You are being asked to work hard at fulfilling your potential.

If the house is so run down that it is in danger of falling apart, the dream may mean that a situation you thought was secure is collapsing, or that you are under severe stress.

A dream about moving into a new house reveals that you are ready to leave your comfort zone and find out more about who and what you are. If it's an unexpectedly grand place, the message is that you have a wealth of inner resources at your disposal. Moving to a house that's less desirable than the one you've left suggests that you are feeling unnecessarily bad about your current lifestyle. You need to appreciate the advantages you have rather than focusing on what you think is lacking.

A dream set in your childhood home usually implies a need to come to terms with emotional issues dating back to the time you lived there.

Questions to ask yourself –
and what to do when the answer is 'yes'

Am I harbouring negative attitudes?
● One good way to start 'repairing' your inner house is to forgive past wrongs. Your dream is urging you to focus on what's positive in your life, to cherish your relationships and to let go of resentment.

Are my stress levels high?
● Your dream is urging you to create a better balance in your life. This could mean booking yourself a massage, practising yoga, meditation or a martial art, or planning a relaxing break.

Do I need to work on myself?
● Many people benefit from self-help books. 'Renovating' your sense of identity though, is difficult to do by yourself. A course of therapy or personal development workshops could help you to put your inner house in order. This is also the best way to tackle outstanding emotional issues dating back to your childhood.

The outside of a house symbolizes the façade you present to the world.

Bathroom

Possible meanings

A bathroom is associated with cleansing and, in symbolic language, implies purification. Your dream may therefore be urging you to deal with negative emotions, attitudes or habits that are preventing you from reaching your full potential.

An alternative meaning is that you need to 'wash away' the opinions or attitudes of other people that you've unthinkingly adopted as your own.

Questions to ask yourself – and what to do when the answer is 'yes'

Am I inclined to be negative?

● If you tend to see the glass as half-empty rather than as half-full, you need to cultivate a more optimistic outlook. Since your destiny is in large part determined by your attitudes, experiences that seem negative can turn out to be opportunities in disguise if you are willing to look for them. It's time to clean up your act and start creating the conditions for a more productive, fulfilling life.

Do I accept other people's views uncritically?

● Nowadays we are subjected to a constant barrage of information via television, newspapers and the internet. This can substantially affect the way you view the world, yet much of what you read and hear bears little resemblance to the truth. It's important to keep your wits about you. If you want to do justice to yourself as an intelligent human being, you need to think things through carefully and listen to the voice of your own intuition.

A bathroom suggests a need to cleanse yourself of toxic emotions.

Toilet

Possible meanings

You dream that you are frantically looking for a toilet, but they are all either out of order or too dirty to use. Even when you find one that works, it has inadequate walls or no door, leaving you exposed to public gaze.

The urge to relieve ourselves is a natural function over which we have only limited control. Your dream therefore suggests a need for genuine, spontaneous self-expression. Dirty toilets imply that you allow other people's needs to take priority over your own.

The inability to find a private toilet indicates that you find it difficult to create an adequate boundary between yourself and the outside world. You are reluctant to express your real feelings for fear of being judged.

Excrement often represents something you cannot digest, or a 'shitty' situation in waking life. Since faeces emerge from within us, they can also symbolize creativity. Sometimes, excrement signifies the darker side of your nature that you'd rather not know about.

Dreaming about a toilet could mean you need to release pent-up emotions.

Questions to ask yourself – and what to do when the answer is 'yes'

Do I tend to subordinate my needs to those of others?
● Your dream is urging you to express yourself more forcefully. Yet this is problematic unless you have the confidence to stand up for yourself. A course of assertiveness training or a class in public speaking could help you to overcome your inhibitions.

Do I suppress my real feelings for fear of being judged?
● The dream also implies that there is an aspect of yourself which you can't accept and that you therefore expect other people to reject. How can you relax and be yourself when there is a side of your personality that you are reluctant to expose? It's time to accept who you are and to stop caring quite so much about what other people think of you. You'll find that if you cultivate a healthy sense of your own worth, then it will follow that others will value what you have to say.

Do I need to explore my darker side?
● Investigating the side of yourself you find unacceptable is not easy, and needs to be done in a safe, supportive environment. You may want to consider psychotherapy, but other possibilities exist too: art therapy, drama workshops or personal development groups can all be highly effective.

Kitchen

Dreams set in a kitchen imply that a process of transformation is occuring.

Possible meanings

Since the kitchen is the room in which we turn raw food into nourishing meals, your dream indicates transformation in some area of your life. Perhaps you're cooking up a plan or a project, or undergoing a change of attitude to someone or something.

Traditionally, the kitchen was considered the heart of the home. A dream about a chaotic kitchen therefore suggests that you need to clear up a messy emotional situation.

If you are cooking for others in your dream the message is that you have a need to nurture or to be of service.

Questions to ask yourself – and what to do when the answer is 'yes'

Is something 'cooking' in some area of my life?

● A successful recipe involves carefully chosen ingredients to which you apply just the right amount of heat. This translates into using your powers of discrimination and drawing on your knowledge and experience. Add a large pinch of inspiration and you have the perfect dish!

Is my attitude to something or somebody changing?

● There are bound to be periods in your life when your perceptions of people and situations change. This is an inevitable part of your psychological development. Your dream is reassuring you that this is a positive process – whatever the outcome.

Do I need to clean up an emotional mess?

● There is a limit to what you as an individual can do to heal a situation in which others are also involved. You can't change other people, but you can take responsibility for your own attitudes. I recommend that you try to avoid taking things personally and do your best to be compassionate. Then your effect on the situation can only be positive.

Do I feel a need to help others?

● In today's world, where so many people need a helping hand, you should have no trouble fulfilling your needs, whether in a professional or a voluntary capacity. Please remember, though, that charity begins at home. Are you serving your nearest and dearest as well as you can?

Cellar

Possible meanings

Since a cellar is below ground level it represents your unconscious mind, the place where you store old memories and entrenched beliefs that determine your actions and choices. This means that whatever you find there symbolizes a repressed side of yourself that you need to become familiar with. Your dream may therefore reveal the underlying causes of a current difficulty.

Dreams that feature cellars can be scary. Who knows what could be lurking down in the darkness? People sometimes say they're afraid of exploring their psychic depths, in case they find something they'd rather not know about. Yet we all have a dark side. It's part of being human, and pretending it doesn't exist can create serious problems in relationships. On a lighter note, cellars can also contain hidden treasures!

Questions to ask yourself –
and what to do when the answer is 'yes'

Do I need to understand why a current problem has developed?
● Your current difficulties are the result of past experience that has deeply influenced you. This means that you need to turn the spotlight on your motives for making the choices that have created problems for you.

Am I afraid of looking at repressed feelings or memories?
● Uncovering something you've tried to suppress is a serious matter. I highly recommend that you seek professional help with this challenging task. Once you're free from the burden of secrecy, you will set in motion your own natural powers of healing.

Is there an aspect of myself that I need to get to know?
● Your dream is encouraging you to draw more deeply on your inner resources. The best way to start is by getting to know more about whatever you find in the cellar, whether it's a person, an animal or an object. You'll find some suggestions about how to do this in the section on Bringing your dreams alive (see page 8).

An exciting discovery in a cellar suggests you have discovered hidden gifts.

Attic

Clutter in an attic could imply a need to clear your mind.

Possible meanings

Since the attic is at the top of the house, it is associated with matters of the mind. Your dream is therefore concerned with your ideas, attitudes or spiritual aspirations.

Discovering an attic can have exciting implications for your waking life. You are on the verge of enjoying new insight or finding fresh inspiration. The section on Finding a new room (see page 92) will help you to understand more about this dream.

Being locked in an attic suggests that you are imprisoned in an overly intellectual approach to life, more at ease with your own thoughts than relating to others. Your dream is encouraging you to come out of your shell and participate more fully in life.

A bare attic is inviting you to furnish your mind with new ideas, interests or creative activities. An attic filled with junk indicates a need to question old, outworn beliefs that limit your horizons.

Questions to ask yourself – and what to do when the answer is 'yes'

Do I feel as though my outlook is changing?
● A change of perspective will help you to approach a current situation in a new and fresh way. You can help this process to unfold by being prepared to follow unusual lines of thought.

Do I tend to live in my head?
● It's fine to enjoy the life of the mind, but your dream suggests that you long for greater emotional fulfilment. A relatively painless way of making new relationships would be to join a group of people with whom you share similar interests.

Do I have too many ideas buzzing round my head?
● You would find it useful to make a list of all the things you're hoping to do, together with a note of how each could enhance your life. Then choose the one that would be most beneficial and focus your mental energy on ways of bringing it about.

Am I limited by old, ingrained attitudes?
● In childhood you were conditioned by the beliefs and opinions of those around you. Now it's time to assess how you were taught to see the world. Would your life be more satisfying with different expectations?

Bedroom

Possible meanings

As you would expect, a dream about a bedroom usually relates to sexual matters or intimate relationships. A cold, unattractive or chaotic bedroom indicates problems in this respect, whilst a newly decorated bedroom can suggest a change of heart. You may be embarking on a new relationship or entering a new phase of an existing one.

It's also possible that your dream concerns a professional partnership or a business deal.

Questions to ask yourself – and what to do when the answer is 'yes'

Am I concerned about the sexual side of a relationship?
● Sexual problems are often the result of lack of communication. Perhaps you are a very private person who finds any form of intimacy challenging. If so your dream is encouraging you to learn to share your thoughts and feelings, as well as your body. It's also possible that one of you is harbouring unexpressed anger or resentment. The sooner you clear the air, the greater the like-lihood of resuming a fulfilling sex life. You could benefit from marriage guidance, whether or not you are actually married.

Am I involved in a business deal or having problems in a professional partnership?
● If you are thinking of 'getting into bed' with someone, your dream may be urging caution. You need to be prepared for unexpected hitches. If you are having difficulties with a colleague, it's important to maintain a professional approach. Maintaining a cool but courteous attitude can help to defuse a potentially explosive situation.

A freshly made bed suggests a new phase in a relationship.

Finding a new room

Possible meanings

You suddenly see a door in your house that you hadn't noticed before. Opening it, you are amazed to find a spacious room you hadn't realized was there. This important dream implies that you have unexplored potential. You are being invited to wake up to hitherto undreamed-of possibilities and make changes in your life.

The dream can occur if you are involved in a new relationship that is unlocking emotions you didn't know you had. If you have just become a parent it may reflect a new sense of self, or powerful feelings of love that have taken you by surprise.

An empty room suggests that your horizons are expanding. This could mean discovering new talents and abilities, furthering your career or exploring new dimensions within your spiritual life. If the room needs cleaning or decorating, the dream carries a message about the need to prepare yourself, mentally or emotionally, for new developments. You may find further clues to the meaning in the following discussion about Furniture (see page 94).

If you come across a door that you cannot open, however hard you try, your dream is urging you to find a way of unlocking hidden potential. A room that you're afraid to enter though usually represents suppressed feelings relating to a traumatic experience.

Questions to ask yourself –
and what to do when the answer is 'yes'

Am I involved in a new relationship?
● You may be discovering a capacity for intimacy or joy that you've never experienced before. At the same time, venturing into new emotional territory can create moments of extreme insecurity. It would be wrong to allow these feelings to spoil the potential for fulfilment that the relationship offers. You can keep them under control by refusing to indulge in fantasies about being rejected. Keep your focus on what's actually happening rather than what you fear might happen.

Am I prepared for new developments?

● It's time to stop dwelling on memories of bad experiences and to let go of toxic emotions like bitterness. Only then will you be ready to embrace new opportunities for happiness. As you open your heart and mind to new developments, longstanding problems may suddenly seem less important.

Have I suppressed some painful feelings?

● Coming to terms with a traumatic experience almost always means dismantling your defences and exposing yourself to the emotions you have tried so hard to avoid. It would be best to seek help from a therapist to uncover an area of your past that now needs healing.

This usually signifies an opportunity to unlock more of your potential.

Furniture

Possible meanings

Furniture symbolizes the attitudes and beliefs that furnish your inner 'psychic house'. A dream set in a sparsely furnished room implies a need to develop the side of yourself that the room represents. A bare living room, for instance, suggests a lack of warmth in your social life. You need to counteract this by making an effort to be more gregarious. You'll find details of other rooms elsewhere in this section.

Perhaps the furniture reminds you of your childhood, the period when you began to acquire your beliefs about who you are and of what you are capable. In this case, your dream could be a message about the need to question some of these long-held attitudes.

Old-fashioned furniture often suggests a tendency to live in the past. However, it can also imply a yearning for the kind of lifestyle that the furniture represents.

Questions to ask yourself –
and what to do when the answer is 'yes'

Do I need to develop some aspect of my personality?
● It may be time to pursue further education, find a more challenging job, or explore your creative abilities. On the other hand, it could simply be that you are lazy and need to be more disciplined.

Is my view of myself too limited?
● Your dream is encouraging you to challenge your assumptions about who and what you are. Perhaps you grew up with the idea that you were not particularly clever or creative. Maybe you were discouraged from pursuing a dream because your parents or teachers thought you lacked talent. If there's something you passionately want to do, or be, the only person who can now stop you is – you.

Do I tend to live in the past?
● Our modern world may be imperfect, but for the majority of people life has never been easy. When you fantasize about the past, do you ever stop to think how you would have fared had you been poor, or ill, or unconventional? Your dream is urging you to tackle an attitude that cannot benefit you, emotionally or spiritually.

Furniture symbolizes the thoughts and attitudes that occupy your mind.

Window

Possible meanings

A window is a metaphor for your outlook on life. Your dream is therefore alerting you to the need for a change of perspective. A dirty window suggests that you're not looking clearly at a situation.

If you're looking in through the window of somebody else's house, it may be that you are trying to gain insight into their thoughts and feelings. Perhaps you are a little too focused on their concerns and need to concentrate instead on your own.

Looking out of a window at something you long to be part of indicates that you have built an invisible barrier around yourself. Yet, deep down, you long to participate more fully in life.

Opening a window often implies a need to be more receptive to outside influences, or to allow others a glimpse into your inner world. However, your dream could also be encouraging you to take advantage of a window of opportunity that will not stay open indefinitely.

An open window can suggest a need to look outwards into the world.

Questions to ask yourself –
and what to do when the answer is 'yes'

Am I obsessed with what somebody is thinking or feeling?

● If the relationship is not going the way you want it to, you may be hoping to improve matters by focusing in minute detail on the inner workings of the other person's mind. In doing so, though, you are sending yourself a subliminal message that your own needs and wishes are less important. You would feel much better if you were to find ways of making your own life more full and interesting.

Do I put up defences against getting too closely involved?

● At some stage in your life, you undoubtedly had good reason to keep people at a distance. Maybe you were trying to protect yourself from the full impact of a traumatic experience. Now that your emotional barrier has served its purpose, it needs dismantling so you can be free to enjoy the fulfilment you deserve. This is a delicate, potentially painful task, and I highly recommend that you seek professional help.

Do people find me uncommunicative?

● Just as opening a window allows fresh air to circulate, inviting someone to step a little way into your inner world could be intellectually or emotionally invigorating. You don't have to bare your soul. You just need to reveal a little more of what's going on in your heart and mind.

Your dream body

Subconsciously, you can be aware of a health challenge long before your waking mind has noticed that something is wrong. This means that a dream featuring a part of your body sometimes provides advance warning of a developing physical problem. A dream in which you are finding it hard to breathe, for instance, may indicate an underlying lung disorder. If you think there's any likelihood of this, you would be wise to see your doctor.

However, your body is also a rich source of metaphors for feelings or attitudes. On a symbolic level, your dream about breathing problems could indicate that you are under pressure and need some breathing space. Almost any area of your body can have symbolic significance: think of embracing a situation wholeheartedly, losing your head over somebody, or putting your best foot forward. In this section I discuss the healing effects of some common dreams featuring parts of the body.

Hands and arms

Possible meanings

Your hands give you the ability to be effective. A dream in which they are tied or wounded can therefore imply that you are not handling a situation well, or finding it hard to grasp an idea or an opportunity.

Your hands are also a means of self-expression, so your dream may be saying something about your creativity. A further meaning is that you need to get in touch with someone, or offer them a helping hand. The dream can also mean that someone is offering you the hand of friendship. This could be a timely healing experience.

Arms have similar symbolic meanings: they can also signify a need to keep someone at arm's length – or to embrace that person more fully.

Questions to ask yourself – and what to do when the answer is 'yes'

Do I feel as though my hands are tied?
● Feeling helpless or ineffectual is often due to lack of communication. Finding the courage to express your feelings will make you feel more powerful and could open up new possibilities. If you feel you're being emotionally blackmailed, it's essential to keep a firm grip on the situation.

Am I aware of handling something badly?
● If this is a work-related issue, and you lack an essential skill, you would benefit from further training. However, if your dream concerns a personal or professional relationship, it's inviting you to try and embrace the other person's point of view.

Do I need to be more creative?
● If you long to acquire a specific skill, it would be good to look for a suitable class. However, creativity is also an attitude of mind. Your dream may therefore be encouraging you to explore different ways of doing familiar things.

Am I out of touch with someone or something?
● If your dream refers to a relationship, it is encouraging you to reach out to the other person, whether verbally, or via a letter or email. Doing so could prevent a conflict developing or heal an existing rift. The response could prove unexpectedly rewarding. A further, quite different meaning is that you need to educate yourself in an area where your lack of knowledge is holding you back.

Hands can signify a need to get a grip on something.

Feet and Legs

Possible meanings

Feet in dreams often signify your standpoint. They can also represent your ability to step forward into a situation. Dreams about problems with feet may therefore imply feelings of insecurity. Perhaps you're unsure of how you stand on an issue, or maybe you're getting cold feet because something isn't working out in the way you expected. It's possible, too, that you're reluctant to take the next step and move on. Sometimes dreams about feet reflect concerns about being wrong-footed.

Since it's through your feet that you make contact with the earth, the dream could also be saying something about the need to be well-grounded in reality.

Since legs are your body's support system, they often symbolize self-reliance. An injured leg may reflect difficulties in being independent, whilst a leg that's missing suggests either that you feel unsupported or that you don't have a leg to stand on.

Your legs are your means of moving on, so a dream in which you find it hard to walk usually relates to a situation in your waking life that seems to be hard going.

Questions to ask yourself –
and what to do when the answer is 'yes'

Am I unsure about where I stand on something?
● It would be good to tell yourself that it's perfectly alright to be unsure. Perhaps you don't yet have enough information and need further discussion with those involved. The dream could also be inviting you to take the initiative in a situation where you have so far been passive.

Am I reluctant to move on?
● It may be that you genuinely need more time to prepare. Otherwise, I suggest you think of ways of rewarding yourself for summoning up the courage to take the next step.

Do I find it hard to be independent?
● Taking responsibility for yourself can be a huge challenge, but you owe it to yourself to live life in your own way. A course of assertiveness training could be invaluable. Another possibility is to set yourself a challenge that would make you draw deeply on your inner resources.

Do I feel I lack support?

● Could it be that you've been too proud to admit you need help? Maybe you've been expecting someone to read your mind but have met with no response. It's also possible that you've been looking for support in the wrong place and need to take advice from another source.

Do I feel stuck?

● If you've tried all possible ways of moving forward to no avail, then you may simply have to be patient and wait for circumstances to change.

Do you feel you are ready to take the next step?

Hair

Hair that's hard to control can signify irrepressible sensuality.

Possible meanings

You dream that your hair is a different colour, length or style. Since hair is an important aspect of your image, dreams like this usually imply that you want the world to see you differently. You may be harbouring a desire to appear more colourful and glamorous, or less conventional. It's also possible that you just need to relax and let your hair down!

Abundant hair is a traditional symbol of sexuality or virility, so a dream in which your hair has been cut off can reflect an underlying anxiety about your desirability or your sexual prowess. Or maybe you suddenly realize, to your horror, that your hair is grey or you are going bald. This dream often occurs in mid-life, and suggests concerns about how growing older will affect your sexuality.

In many dreams hair represents the ideas, thoughts, and fantasies that emerge from your head. Are they abundant and colourful, or sparse and dull? If you are combing tangles out of your hair, it could be time to get your ideas straight.

Questions to ask yourself – and what to do when the answer is 'yes'

Am I dissatisfied with the way I look?
● How would you prefer to be seen? If you want to make changes to your appearance, but aren't sure how to go about it, you could benefit from the advice of an image consultant. Whatever you do, it would be as well to remember, though, that what matters most is to feel good about being the person you are.

Am I worried about losing my sex appeal?
● Feeling unattractive or sexually inadequate can be the result of problems you are experiencing in a current relationship. If you've tried to rectify matters but see no hope of improvement, it may be better to accept that the relationship is over than to feel constantly undermined. However, if you have a history of sexual difficulties, you would benefit from consulting a therapist who specializes in this area.

Do I need to pay more attention to my ideas and fantasies?
● Your dream is a message to start exploring your inner life. You could start tapping into your creative energy by turning a fantasy into a story, a painting or a dance.

Eyes

Possible meanings

Since eyes are associated with wisdom and insight, your dream may be encouraging you to trust your vision. An unfriendly, critical eye can reflect the fact that you feel someone is judging you. It could also represent your own inner judge which is making you feel that your way of seeing things is wrong or foolish.

Eyes often feature in a dream if you're having to keep an eye on someone or something in waking life. Poor vision suggests a need to focus more clearly on the job in hand. However, it may also indicate that there's something you'd prefer not to see.

A dream about eyes may be inviting you to observe a situation more closely.

Questions to ask yourself – and what to do when the answer is 'yes'

Do I tend to doubt my own perceptions?
● The dream is encouraging you to learn to trust yourself. I recommend that you look at the section of this book on Bringing your dreams alive (see page 8). There you will find suggestions about how to control a harsh inner critic so that you feel free to be spontaneous.

Do I need to keep a close eye on something?
● Cultivating your powers of observation takes practice and patience. First you need to recognize the value of paying close attention to detail. You could find it useful to ask yourself how your favourite fictional detective would approach the situation.

Is there something I'd rather not see?
● Sometimes turning a blind eye is the best way of dealing with a situation. However, if this doesn't seem to be working, you simply have to face facts and start taking appropriate action. Finding the courage to be more proactive will help to heal the part of you that associates confronting reality with pain or danger.

Identity and image

Dreams about clothes or other aspects of your appearance relate to your persona, the image you present to the world. The word 'persona' was originally used to describe the mask an actor wore on stage to indicate which role he was playing. In dreams, your clothing and accessories are the equivalent of the actor's mask. They carry a message about how you see yourself and the way others see you.

Unless you have an adequate persona, you are liable to be easily hurt. A confident image can disguise feelings of inadequacy or camouflage deep wounds. However, it's important to avoid being over-identified with a particular role and the status it brings you. Should that role be threatened your self-esteem will be undermined and you could even succumb to depression.

Dreams about your appearance can help you to develop a stronger sense of identity. In this section you will discover more about their healing potential.

Shoes

Possible meanings

Dreams about shoes usually say something about your standpoint. Shopping for new shoes, for instance, suggests that it's time to look at someone or something, from a different perspective. Shoes that feel too tight tend to signify a need for a broader outlook.

Losing your shoes often implies that you don't know where you stand. Another meaning is also possible. Since shoes fit snugly around your feet, they can be a symbol for female sexuality. Your dream could then reflect a concern about losing touch with your sensual nature.

Walking along without shoes can signify a need to be more carefree and natural. If the ground feels rough beneath your feet, though, the message is that you are currently going through a difficult patch.

A dream about wearing somebody else's shoes may be inviting you to imagine standing in their shoes and experiencing life from their point of view. However, it could also imply that you identify a little too much with this person, and need to develop your own, individual, standpoint.

Questions to ask yourself –
and what to do when the answer is 'yes'

Do I need to cultivate a different attitude to something or somebody?
● Your dream is encouraging you to be more open-minded. Overcoming a prejudice would allow you to make progress in a current situation, or revitalize a relationship.

Am I unsure of where I stand?
● Your dream is urging you to stay connected to your highest values or your personal vision, so that you can step out once more with confidence.

As a woman, do I feel I've lost touch with my more erotic side?
● If your sex life is unfulfilling, you may be suppressing feelings of resentment or anxiety. A therapist or relationship counsellor could help you to communicate more openly with your partner. It may be, though, that you are stressed and need to take a break. Relaxing treatments like massage or aromatherapy would also be beneficial.

Am I finding life hard going?
● One effective way of softening the impact of harsh reality is to imagine you are surrounded by a protective cocoon of light. Another is to pretend you are wearing a plastic skin that stops unpleasant experiences from affecting you too deeply.

A woman's dream of well-fitting shoes can mean she's comfortable with her sexuality.

Clothes

Possible meanings

A dream that features clothing provides insight into the changes you may need to make to your persona. Wearing something uncomfortably tight indicates that the image you present to the world is too limiting. A side of yourself that you tend to hide is bursting to get out and make its presence felt.

Shabby old clothing represents outworn attitudes or old habits that you need to change, whilst black clothes can signify a desire to be anonymous. Shopping for new clothes indicates that you're trying to create a different image or hoping to make a fresh start.

A dream featuring the clothes you usually wear for work can reflect the way you feel about your job. If they are falling apart, for instance, the dream could indicate that you are disenchanted with your job and tired of keeping up a façade. If, though, you are at a party or on holiday in your working clothes, the message is that you are over-identified with your professional role.

An outfit that's too informal for the occasion suggests that you are reluctant to conform. Being over-dressed, on the other hand, means you need to loosen up a little.

Wearing somebody else's clothes implies that you are modelling yourself too much on him or her, instead of creating an image that suits your own individual personality.

Perhaps someone in the dream has made a disparaging remark about your outfit, implying that it's too revealing, for instance, or too youthful for someone of your age. This suggests you have a conflict between your wish to project a certain image and your fear of being seen as attention-seeking, or mutton dressed as lamb.

Questions to ask yourself – and what to do when the answer is 'yes'

Do I keep a side of myself firmly under wraps?
● It's sometimes wise to hide your true feelings, but you'd find life more enjoyable if you could allow yourself to be a little less inhibited.

Do I find it hard to switch off from work?

● Most jobs require a focused, goal-oriented attitude. For the sake of maintaining a healthy emotional balance, it's important to do something non-competitive in your leisure time. Activities like gardening, sewing, or cooking, or anything you enjoy doing for its own sake could help to relax you, physically and mentally.

Do I tend to imitate somebody I admire?

● When you're unsure of yourself it can be helpful to have a role model. Long-term though, you need to develop the confidence to trust your own judgment. If you are willing to experiment, you will soon start discovering your own, unique style.

Am I worried that people would disapprove if I changed my image?

● It would be a pity to let your fear of disapproval stop you from expressing a more adventurous side of your personality. You may feel more confident if you ask a good friend to be with you when you first appear in public in your new guise.

Choosing new clothes in a dream is linked to searching for a different image.

Jewellery

The circular shape of a ring often represents a sense of fulfilment.

Possible meanings

Jewellery is a metaphor for valuable qualities such as wisdom, integrity or self-respect. Dreams about losing jewellery can therefore imply a sense of being diminished by circumstances in your waking life. Since jewellery can symbolize a woman's sexuality, this dream could also suggest you feel cheap, perhaps as a result of being too free with your favours. If someone you know gives you an item of jewellery, the dream may be telling you that he or she values you more highly than you realize.

Some dreams feature a specific item of jewellery, often a ring. This is a traditional symbol of wholeness, and can indicate a well-rounded person-ality or a deep desire for fulfilment. If the ring is lost or damaged, you may be feeling betrayed or disappointed because your relationship has failed to meet your expectations.

Questions to ask yourself – and what to do when the answer is 'yes'

Do I feel devalued in some respect?
● If you're in a situation that's threatening your integrity, it's important to find a way out as soon as possible. If, though, your lack of self-worth is con-tributing to the problem, you need to focus on building your confidence.

As a woman, do I need to discriminate more in choosing sexual partners?
● Sleeping around may offer temporary satisfaction but can damage your self-respect. If you want a fulfiling relationship, you need to value yourself more highly. You also need to take time to discover what a prospective partner can bring to the relationship.

Am I disappointed in my relationship?
● It may be that your expectations were too high. Before you give up on the relationship, it would be wise to see a counsellor to discuss your situation. If you then decide to split up with your partner, you will at least embark upon your next relationship with a more realistic attitude – and a greater chance of finding happiness.

Do I feel my partner has betrayed me?
● It's easy to blame the other person, much harder to acknowledge that you, too, may have played a part in creating the situation. Perhaps you have taken your partner for granted or failed to express your feelings. Your dream is warning you against thinking of yourself as a hapless victim.

Money

Possible meanings

Money in dreams signifies value, energy or inner resources. A dream about being robbed therefore suggests that you feel devalued or taken for granted. It could also be warning you that someone is depleting you emotionally. Losing money can indicate feelings of worthlessness, or a suspicion that you have sold yourself short.

Perhaps you dream that you go to pay a bill, only to find that all your money has disappeared or become worthless. This suggests that you have a wealth of inner resources but are unable to draw on them. Perhaps you find it hard to believe you have anything of real value to offer. Alternatively, your dream may reflect a fear that you don't have what it takes to reach a goal or realize an ambition.

Questions to ask yourself –
and what to do when the answer is 'yes'

Do I feel I'm not appreciated?
● Other people tend to pick up subliminally what you think about yourself. They then react to you accordingly. This means that if you want to be valued, it's essential to value yourself.

Do I find someone's company exhausting?
● You are probably giving too much for too little return and need to be more assertive. It may be best to spend less time with this person.

Am I selling myself short?
● Reluctance to place a proper value on yourself or your work implies that, deep down, you feel inadequate. Feelings like this often date back to childhood. Since children thrive on praise you can heal those old wounds by constantly telling yourself how well you are doing.

Do I feel I have nothing of value to contribute?
● You may need to distance yourself from a situation that's undermining your confidence. If, though, you have a poor sense of self-worth, you would benefit from developing a skill, or volunteering your services to a local hospital, or other organization. The more you draw on your resources, the more confident you will feel.

Am I worried that I won't achieve something I've set my heart on?
● You'll be more likely to succeed if you can enjoy the process of aiming for your goal rather than worrying about the outcome.

A dream about having plenty of money suggests a healthy sense of self-worth.

Handbag

Possible meanings

You have lost your handbag and are desperately looking for it, or you realize, to your horror, that it has been stolen. More than one meaning for these dreams is possible.

Most handbags contain personal items like keys, make-up and money, together with some form of identification. Losing your bag can therefore suggest you are feeling insecure about your identity. This dream often coincides with a major change of circumstances, such as the end of a relationship, retirement or being made redundant.

Since a woman's handbag is often used for carrying valuable possessions, it can also symbolize her womb. If your children have left home and you are therefore suffering from 'empty nest syndrome', losing your bag reflects an underlying anxiety about losing your worth as a woman. A handbag can also represent the female genitalia, in which case your dream reveals concerns about your sexuality. Women in poor relationships, or who have reached the menopause, often have dreams like this.

Not all dreams about handbags involve losing it. Finding or being given another woman's handbag suggests that you are looking for a role model to emulate, in the hope that this will give you a sense of identity or self-worth.

Questions to ask yourself –
and what to do when the answer is 'yes'

Has a change of circumstances undermined my sense of identity?
● I suggest you try to think of the situation not as an obstacle to your happiness, but as a stepping-stone to a fulfilling new phase. Your new circumstances are challenging you to open your mind to new possibilities. It's important to persuade yourself that focusing on the past will make you feel worse, not better. The sooner you can accept your current reality, the stronger and more optimistic you will feel.

Am I afraid I am losing my worth as a woman?
● If you have always defined yourself as a mother, your dream is a message that you now need to expand your areas of interest. You could use your need to nurture for the benefit of the wider community, perhaps by doing voluntary work. Learning a new skill would also help to increase your confidence. If you are worried about losing your sex

appeal, remember that your attitude is more important than your physical attributes. A woman who radiates confidence, is interested in others and loves life will always be attractive, whatever her age.

Am I trying to model myself on somebody else?

● It's fine to cultivate the qualities you admire in another person but to try and be that person is to do yourself an injustice. If you feel inhibited about expressing yourself in your own, individual way, a course of assertiveness training, or classes in a creative activity like art or drama could help to heal your sense of inadequacy.

Problems with your handbag imply that you feel insecure about your identity.

Rites of passage

Indigenous peoples traditionally marked milestones like puberty, marriage, menopause and death with ceremonies designed to help the participants adapt to their new circumstances. With the support of the whole community they could then let go of the past and move forward wholeheartedly into the new phase, whether in this life or the next.

In our materialistically rich but spiritually impoverished culture we have few meaningful rites of passage. No amount of expensive designer gear can help a teenage boy to make the transition to manhood. The most lavish retirement gift will not prepare the recipient to accept his or her new status as a wise elder.

Fortunately our dreams are there to provide us with a resource that meets this essential healing function. Take their messages seriously, and they will guide you safely into the next phase of your life.

Birth

Possible meanings

You suddenly realize you are pregnant and about to give birth – or maybe you have a baby but you don't remember being pregnant. A dream like this can sometimes simply indicate the desire to have a baby.

Usually though it has a more symbolic meaning that applies equally to men and women. Birth can be a metaphor for a new side of your nature that is about to emerge, such as an ability you hadn't realized you possessed. Alternatively, you could be incubating an idea or project that is now coming to fruition, possibly nine months after it was originally conceived.

Giving birth can also indicate renewal in some area of your life. The dream could refer to an improvement in your health, a change of circumstances, a new relationship or even a feeling of being reborn after a period of stagnation.

If the pregnancy has lasted a long time but there's no sign of a baby, the dream suggests that you have been hoping to find fulfilment through something that has failed to materialize. It could also allude to a relationship that has never quite taken off.

Birth is often the metaphor for the start of a new phase.

Questions to ask yourself – and what to do when the answer is 'yes'

Am I trying to develop an idea or a project?
● Your dream is encouraging you to be patient. There is no point in trying to force progress as your unconscious mind is working on your plans and will bring them to fruition, but not a moment before it is ready.

Am I experiencing a new lease of life?
● Your feelings in the dream reflect your attitude to the new situation in your waking life. Whether you are overjoyed, astonished or scared to find you're giving birth, you need to embrace the new developments and nurture them as best you can.

Am I disappointed because something I'd hoped for just isn't happening?
● Although your feelings are understandable, I recommend that you waste no further effort on something that is clearly not going to fulfil its promise. It would be much better to find a new direction for your energy.

Weddings

Possible meanings

You're walking up the aisle on your wedding day when you realize your prospective spouse is nowhere in sight. If you are about to get married, your dream simply reflects pre-wedding nerves. You can also have this dream if you are thinking about marriage but aren't yet ready to tie the knot. However, a deeper meaning is also possible.

A wedding often signifies the union of the masculine and feminine sides of your nature. If the bridegroom is missing, your dream is encouraging you to develop your masculine qualities, such as the ability to be focused, assertive or coolly objective. A missing bride implies a need to get in touch with the tender, sensitive, intuitive side of your nature.

Of course, not all dreams about weddings feature a missing partner. Perhaps you're marrying someone you know but would never, in your waking life, consider as a partner. Nevertheless, dreaming about them in this way suggests that he or she embodies a quality or an attitude that you need to find within yourself.

Dreaming about marrying one of your parents does not automatically imply that you are harbouring incestuous fantasies. It could – but it can also mean that you are a mother's boy or that your heart belongs to daddy, so you are not ready to make a commitment.

Wearing inappropriate clothes can reflect your subconscious hopes and feelings about marriage. If you are dressed in black, for instance, a colour more usually associated with mourning, you may not associate marriage with happiness.

Questions to ask yourself –
and what to do when the answer is 'yes'

Am I out of touch with my masculine or feminine energy?
● Your undeveloped masculine side could respond to further education, or an activity such as chess or archery that needs focused concentration. If you're out of touch with your feminine energy, you can remedy this by putting some more effort into your relationships or spending more time with your children.

Do I need to cultivate qualities with which I don't usually identify?
● Your dream marks a milestone in your psychological development. You have got more potential than you think and you are now ready to draw on it. If there's something you suspect you could be or do, then now is the time to start.

Do I prefer one of my parents to anybody else?

● One of the signs of maturity is the ability to love your parents without being over-dependent on them. If you idealize your mother or father, you will subconsciously expect a prospective partner to live up to impossibly high expectations. Your dream is therefore urging you to cut the umbilical cord and venture out into the wider world of relationships.

Do I feel marriage is not for me?

● There's no law that says you have to get married. Could it be, though, that your attitude is the result of your experience of your parents' relationship? Perhaps they seemed unhappy or frustrated. Yet many people find marriage deeply fulfilling despite its inevitable ups and downs.

A wedding may symbolize a desire to find life-long love and devotion.

Retirement

Possible meanings

Retirement is a major 'rite of passage', when it becomes psychologically and spiritually appropriate to focus less on the material world and more on your inner life. Recurring dreams about being back in your old workplace suggest that you are finding it difficult to adjust to this new phase.

Perhaps you are bewildered because nothing is as it used to be or people are surprised to see you there. Many variations on this theme are possible, but they all tend to raise issues such as: 'What is my status now?' and 'If I don't know where I fit in, how can I be of use?'. The setting of your dreams implies that you are looking to the past for your answers.

Your dream could also suggest that you took your former responsibilities so much to heart that, subconsciously, you are still carrying them.

Questions to ask yourself – and what to do when the answer is 'yes'

Do I miss the status my job gave me?

● One of the joys of retirement is that it provides the opportunity to reassess your priorities. Now there's no longer anything you're obliged to achieve, you can find out what really matters to you. If you can see the next phase of your life as a time for exploring new possibilities, your self-respect will soon return.

Does my life seem empty now?

● When you finished work, you took with you inner resources developed over many years. Although your circumstances have changed, you still possess deep reserves of experience on which to draw. Can you identify the qualities that you acquired during your working life? Do you value them sufficiently? Could you use these qualities in a different context, such as voluntary work or mentoring young people? Try to see yourself as an elder who can guide others, not someone who has been tossed onto the scrapheap of life.

Do I ask too much of myself?

● If you are too much of a perfectionist, you will torment yourself by never feeling good enough. Your dreams are urging you to forgive yourself for your perceived shortcomings and to accept that you have always done your best. You could tell yourself a hundred times a day, especially before you go to sleep, what a worthwhile person you are.

Dreams of your workplace may show you're emotionally unprepared for retirement.

Death

Possible meanings

If someone you love is very ill, dreaming about their death can be nature's way of preparing you for the inevitable. Otherwise dreams about death have a symbolic, not a literal meaning.

A dream about the death of a loved one can imply an underlying fear of being abandoned or rejected. It could also suggest an inner conflict between your love for this person and other quite different feelings like guilt or resentment, that make you want to be free of the relationship.

Sometimes a dream about the death of a partner or friend means that the relationship has run its course.

A dream in which your child dies may be urging you to take better care of a child-like, vulnerable side of your self. An alternative meaning is that you are overanxious for your child's welfare. You can also have this dream when your child starts growing up.

Dreaming about your own death usually indicates a need for a totally different attitude or a radical transformation in your circumstances.

Perhaps you've dreamt about holding a conversation with a deceased person. Sceptics would argue that this is mere wish-fulfilment. In my experience though, a dream visitor often brings a special message of comfort, or guidance that can heal grief overnight or miraculously transform a bereaved person's attitude to death.

Questions to ask yourself –
and what to do when the answer is 'yes'

Do I sometimes long to be free of a relationship?
● Successful relationships thrive on negotiation, so it's essential to address your frustrations, not just allow them to build up and fester.

Do I feel as though a part of me has died?
● It may be that certain values or beliefs you used to find important are no longer relevant. However, if you have neglected an important aspect of your personality the dream is inviting you to revive it. In what way would your life need to change so that this part of you could come alive again?

Do I feel as though a situation is killing me?
● If you can't, or don't want to, extricate yourself from the situation, you must at least find some way of taking better care of your own interests. Friends could be a valuable source of support, but I strongly urge you to seek professional help.

A dead person can represent an aspect of yourself that has 'died'.

Animals

Like all animals, we are programmed to ensure the survival of our species by seeking food, reproducing ourselves and protecting our young. Animals in dreams therefore tend to represent our deepest instincts. We can pay attention to these, as we might nurture a pet. Or we can disregard them, as we might ignore a creature with which we feel no empathy.

A poor relationship with your instincts can lead to health problems, so a dream about being on bad terms with an animal may be trying to help you avoid illness.

Wild animals often symbolize dangerous, uncontrolled emotions or destructive forces. They can also reveal your uncensored reactions to people or situations. Or perhaps you've been lucky enough to have a dream about a magical, talking creature. This comparatively rare dream brings a healing message from your inmost self.

Lions

Possible meanings

Lions signify nobility and, of course, pride. A dream about struggling with a lion may be encouraging you to wrestle with a tendency you may have to be too proud or egocentric.

Lions copulate for long periods at a time, so they are also associated with sexual passion. You may therefore find you have dreams of being chased by a lion if you are in a sexually unfulfilling relationship. Sometimes, though, a dream like this can reflect a voracious sexual appetite that is out of control.

As 'king of the jungle', a lion symbolizes leadership and can signify a need to take the initiative in a situation where you're being passive. If you are afraid of asserting yourself in case your feelings get out of hand, the lion may embody suppressed feelings of rage.

A dream that features a lioness stalking her prey is encouraging you to exercise patience and concentration in aiming for a goal. For the time being, it would be best to maintain a low profile.

Questions to ask yourself –
and what to do when the answer is 'yes'

Do I need to be more lion-like in some aspect of my life?
● Current circumstances are challenging you to maintain your dignity or demonstrate qualities such as courage or generosity. If pride is creating conflict, the dream is urging you to cultivate a courteous heart.

Am I in a sexually unfulfilling relationship?
● Your dream is encouraging you to find ways of retrieving some loving 'jungle magic'. Maybe you need to invest in some sex aids, an adult video or two or a stimulating book. Since the underlying problem is often lack of communication, the situation may improve if you spend more time discussing your thoughts and feelings with each other.

Am I suppressing feelings of anger?
● Since your dream is urging you to be more assertive, you could find it helpful to practise embodying 'lion energy'. Try getting down on all fours and moving like a lion. If you're physically unable to do this you can move on to the next step, which is to practise roaring! This is an excellent way of releasing the tension that builds up in your throat whenever you swallow your rage.

A lion personifies courage, dignity and majestic power.

Cats

Possible meanings

Cats have many different symbolic meanings. Since they are extremely fertile they can represent feminine sexuality, the desire for a baby or a need to be creative. If you are pregnant, you may even dream about giving birth to kittens!

Because of their ability to see in the dark, cats have traditionally been associated with intuitive, feminine wisdom. Whether you are male or female, your dream could be encouraging you to listen more carefully to this side of yourself. Dreams in which you realize you've forgotten to feed the cat imply that you are neglecting your inmost feminine nature.

Cats are also sensual, comfort-loving, relaxed and playful creatures. They enjoy life for its own sake and have no need to prove anything. If you are stressed, or tend to be competitive and driven, you may need to embody more of these feline qualities.

Although they are domesticated pets, cats are nevertheless also independent and sure of themselves. They expect you to meet their needs but never seek approval. If you tend to be a 'people-pleaser', your dream is encouraging you to be less accommodating.

Cats have sharp teeth and claws which they don't hesitate to use if they feel aggrieved. In some dreams, then, they signify 'nature, red in tooth and claw'. A dream about an angry, hissing cat may be urging you to show your claws in a situation where your interests are threatened.

Questions to ask yourself – and what to do when the answer is 'yes'

Do I need to cultivate a more relaxed attitude to life?
● This interpretation often applies to the dreams of women who have stressful or high-powered jobs. If a woman is to succeed in a thrusting, go-getting, essentially masculine environment, she has to draw on her focused, goal-oriented, masculine side. Your 'inner man' thrives on a diet of high achievement, but your more receptive, feminine side can suffer unless you make time to switch off and recharge your batteries, allowing yourself time to enjoy 'being' rather than 'doing'. Your dream is urging you to incorporate more relaxing pursuits into your busy life. A regular massage or yoga class would help to redress the balance.

Do I need to nurture my feminine side?

● Depending on your personality, your feminine side may thrive on art, music, dancing, lunching with friends or contact with nature. In fact, anything that you enjoy doing for its own sake will help to meet your needs. If you are stuck in an unfulfilling relationship, your dream is inviting you to consider your options. Perhaps it's time to move on, although it may be worth seeking counselling before making any drastic moves.

Do I need to be more assertive?

● Your cat dream is encouraging you to express your feelings more forcefully. Otherwise, they will fester, making you moody and resentful. Learning a martial art could help you to feel more comfortable about standing up for yourself. Activities like kick-boxing or fencing can also be effective aids to developing assertiveness.

In Ancient Egypt cats were sacred to the goddess of fertility and sensual pleasures.

Snakes

Possible meanings

People often assume that a snake must be a phallic symbol. This is obviously the meaning to consider if you are experiencing sexual problems, or difficulties in expressing the assertive, masculine side of your nature. There are, though, many other possible meanings.

Snakes often represent feminine wisdom, a deep intuitive sense that something is right even if it cannot be proved by rational argument. Many ancient civilizations valued this type of knowledge and depicted it as a goddess wearing or holding snakes.

Another meaning is based on the story of Eve being tempted by a serpent to eat forbidden fruit in the Garden of Eden. In this case, a snake reflects a seductive choice you are being offered in waking life.

The fundamental life-force that practitioners of yoga call 'kundalini' energy is also represented by a serpent. A dream about a wounded snake can therefore imply that your vital energy is seriously depleted.

Sometimes a snake personifies a venomous attitude. Yet it can also signify healing. The Greek god Asclepius, the god of healing, was depicted with a snake – a symbol of the medical profession to this day.

Questions to ask yourself –
and what to do when the answer is 'yes'

Do I have sexual problems?
● You may feel undesirable, perhaps due to rejection. Counselling, self-help books, therapy and medical intervention are all resources that can help.

Do I find it hard to trust my intuition?
● You could benefit from one of the popular workshops now available to help you strengthen this side of your nature. Focusing on your inner voice with a group of like-minded people would give you the confidence to value your insights. You will then find it easier to resist being undermined by arguments that, although logical, somehow miss the point.

Am I exhausted?
● Your dream carries a strong message about the need to relax. Unless you slow down, you could develop health problems.

Do I need healing?
● Your dream is urging you to support your body's own healing powers by maintaining a healthy lifestyle and avoiding excessive stress.

Because it sheds its skin, a snake can symbolize rejuvenation or renewal.

Fish

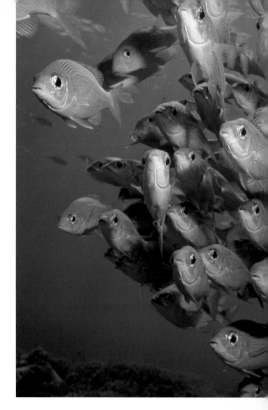

Possible meanings

Fish often symbolize inspiration, or the ideas that we 'fish up' from the depths of our subconscious mind. In Christian symbolism they are a metaphor for eternal life or our true self.

Fish also signify fertility and may feature in your dream if you are hoping to be pregnant. Women undergoing IVF treatment often tell me they have dreams about fish.

Goldfish are usually associated with a domestic environment and issues of stability. Sharks, on the other hand, represent wild, predatory urges within your psyche that could endanger your entire lifestyle if you let them take over.

If your dream makes use of a common metaphor relating to fish, the meaning will become clear once you have understood the play on words. Do you feel like a fish out of water? Are you a big fish in a small pond? Do you have emotional difficulties that make others think of you as a 'cold fish'? Have you been fishing for compliments? Are you involved in a fishy situation that poses a threat to your own best interests?

Fish lay many eggs and can represent sexual drive and the urge to reproduce.

Questions to ask yourself – and what to do when the answer is 'yes'

Am I at a loss for inspiration?

● Inspiration rarely tends to happen when you are anxiously trying to find it. It's best to put yourself into a deep state of relaxation so that your brain waves slow down, allowing deeper layers of the mind to surface. Many people find that going for a long walk is an excellent way of helping the mind to roam free.

Do I need to pay more attention to my spiritual life?

● Since a fish is an important Christian symbol, your dream could be encouraging you to find out what your local church has to offer. You may also want to consider working with a spiritual director or counsellor who could help you to get in touch with the spark of divinity deep within your psyche.

Am I having problems with my sex drive?

● Whether your libido is underactive or working overtime, a great deal of help is available. You could start by consulting your doctor in case you have a hormonal imbalance. If the cause is psychological rather than physical, you would find it beneficial to seek counselling.

Dogs

Possible meanings

As 'man's best friend', dogs symbolize loyalty and companionship. With their highly developed sense of smell, they also represent intuition, which is the faculty that enables you to sniff things out. If your dream features a guide dog, it is encouraging you to follow your instincts rather than your intellect.

A dream about a guard dog suggests a need to be alert to potential danger in a current situation. A playful dog, on the other hand, implies a subconscious desire for a more relaxed, spontaneous approach to life.

Perhaps you have dreams about a black dog, which is a well-known symbol for depression. The meaning is further reinforced if the dog is snarling or barking furiously, since depression is often the result of suppressing feelings of anger. If the dream keeps recurring, it's a message that your subconscious mind is doggedly determined to make you do something about it.

A dog is generally considered a masculine symbol, and can sometimes represent a penis. If the dog in your dream is female though, it may signify bitchiness, whether your own or someone else's.

Questions to ask yourself –
and what to do when the answer is 'yes'

Am I finding it hard to make a decision?
● If you have considered the available choices from all angles, it's time to stop worrying about making the right one and let instinct be your guide. That way, you're more likely to arrive at the outcome you really want, instead of the one you think you ought to want.

Do I need to be alert to potential danger?
● This could mean something as simple as ensuring that your home alarm system is working well. Otherwise you may need to take care that something you are planning to do is truly in your own best interests. It would also be good to question somebody's motives.

Am I depressed?
● Your dream is encouraging you to face up to the need to seek help. I highly recommend you visit your doctor. Excellent treatments are available that would alleviate your anxiety and set you free to enjoy your self, your relationships – and your life.

Could my dream refer to bitchiness?

● If someone is being unpleasant about you it would be good to confront them, perhaps with the help of a friend or family member. Bringing things out into the open may be all that's necessary to improve the situation. If it doesn't, you may have no choice but to distance yourself from this person. If you're the one who's being bitchy, ask yourself what you're gaining by it. Do you actually need to be more assertive?

A vicious dog personifies the destructive power of neglected instincts.

Frogs and toads

Possible meanings

Frogs are associated with water and rain and were traditionally thought to resemble the human foetus. They are therefore a symbol of fertility and can reflect a desire to have children or a need to be more creative. Frogs often feature in the dreams of pregnant women, and can also appear in a man's dream if he needs to develop the protective, caring side of his nature.

Since frogs often hop around for long periods before they settle they can also represent lack of consistency.

If you find the frog repulsive you may need to see the beauty or value in someone or something you consider ugly.

Because of their shape, toads have always been associated with the uterus, so they too can signify maternal instincts. However, a toad can also signify a cold-blooded part of your own nature that you need to keep in check.

Questions to ask yourself – and what to do when the answer is 'yes'

Do I need to explore my creativity?
● It would be useful to ask yourself what's holding you back. If you are worried that you may lack ability, you could set your fears to rest by joining a beginner's class in the skill you want to develop.

As a man, do I need to develop my caring side?
● You could start by following a philosophy of 'do as you would be done by'. The more you practise standing in another person's shoes, the more sensitive you will be to their needs and feelings.

Am I considered unreliable?
● Perhaps you tend to become intensely involved in people and situations for a short time, but then move on to pastures new. It's time to consider the bigger picture. True freedom comes from commitment to a relationship or project through which you can develop your potential.

Do I need to cultivate a more compassionate view of someone?
● What happens if you try to visualize the person in question as a small child? Does he or she have a vulnerable side? Can you identify with this? If you can relate more lovingly to the child, you may find it easier to accept the adult.

Since frogs develop from tadpoles, they can symbolize transformation.

Birds

Possible meanings

Birds represent freedom, flights of fantasy, spiritual yearnings and inspiring thoughts that suddenly pop into your head. If the bird in your dream is caged, you may feel constrained by circumstances and long to take wing.

Soaring birds can symbolize your aspirations, the ability to soar to new heights or a desire to rise above problems. When the bird is injured or dead, it may mean that the hopes you've invested in a relationship or a project have plummeted to earth.

If you are preoccupied with a relationship, two birds in your dream may be 'lovebirds'.

Some birds are a metaphor for a specific aspect of yourself that you need to develop. Think of the dove, traditionally associated with peace and love, or the owl, symbol of wisdom because of its ability to see in the dark. An eagle can embody your high-flying or higher, spiritual nature, or it can represent the need to look at a situation with an 'eagle eye'.

Questions to ask yourself –
and what to do when the answer is 'yes'

Am I feeling inspired?
● Inspiration can fly away as quickly as it came, so your dream is encouraging you to incorporate your thoughts and ideas into whichever aspect of your waking life they could enrich.

Do I long to transcend my current circumstances?
● It may be that, for practical reasons, you need to be grounded at this time. If not, you would find it helpful to identify what's stopping you from taking off. Perhaps you are concerned about the changes this would involve and need to take a leap of faith. It would also be good to check that you are not using your circumstances as an excuse to avoid taking responsibility for yourself.

Have my hopes for a relationship or a project been dashed?
● Please don't despair. However hard we try to get something off the ground, there are times when circumstances are simply against us. It may be the wrong time, the wrong person, the wrong project – or a combination of all of these. The more philosophical you are, the sooner your wounds will heal.

A caged bird indicates a yearning to be a free spirit.

Horses

Possible meanings

Horses often represent your fundamental energy or libido, the 'horse-power' that carries you forward through life. They can also symbolize the formidable strength of your emotions and instincts, especially your sexual drive. A sick horse may therefore signify loss of health, vitality or sexual desire.

A bolting horse personifies emotions that are seriously out of control whereas one that's tightly tethered implies emotional repression.

Horses are often credited with extra-sensory powers, so your dream could be encouraging you to allow your intuition or 'horse sense' to guide you.

A white horse often signifies spiritual awareness, but a dream of a flying, winged horse may imply that you are indulging in flights of fantasy. If you are working too hard, your dream may feature a 'work-horse'.

Questions to ask yourself – and what to do when the answer is 'yes'

Are my energy levels low?
● If your 'horse-power' is not functioning as it should, you may be suffering from lack of motivation and need to reassess your lifestyle. It's also possible that you are more exhausted than you realize. If you don't slow down, you could put your health at risk.

Have I lost interest in sex?
● Perhaps you are feeling so tired or stressed that sex is not a priority. A short break away from home could help to rekindle your romance. Hormonal problems sometimes cause loss of libido, so ask your doctor for the relevant tests. If you're harbouring feelings of resentment towards your partner, you could benefit from relationship counselling.

Are my emotions out of control?
● Discussing your feelings with your family or friends may help to restore your emotional balance. If this is not an option, I recommend you to consult a therapist.

Do I keep my feelings on a tight rein?
● Subconsciously, you may associate losing control with being destructive. Yet suppressed feelings are likely to explode and create havoc and fear. It would be healthier to express your feelings more freely.

A horse can signify intuitive understanding that defies any rational explanation.

Insects

Possible meanings

Insects often symbolize things or people that are bugging you. If you are trying to kill the insects, they could represent aspects of yourself that you find irritating and would prefer to get rid of. Stinging insects signify feelings of being stung by what someone has said.

Flies tend to be associated with dirt and with the devil, so they sometimes symbolize dirty thoughts you are trying to suppress.

Spiders often they indicate a fear of being trapped or rendered powerless, but they can also suggest a tendency to be overly controlling. You can dream about a spider if you have problems with a manipulative mother who entangles you in her web.

Questions to ask yourself –
and what to do when the answer is 'yes'

Is someone or something bugging me?

● If there's nothing you can do to improve matters, you will have to try to be more tolerant. Those annoying bugs could be challenging you to be more creative or proactive, though.

Do I have characteristics I'd like to eradicate?

● Would you consider chopping off bits of your body? This is the physical equivalent of what you'd like to do to your psyche. It's much better to be authentic, warts and all, than to pretend to be somebody you are not. Oddly enough, the more relaxed you are about what you see as your peculiarities, the less they will trouble you.

Am I feeling upset by what someone has said?

● It could be good to confront this person, whether face to face or by letter. If you are unwilling or unable to do this, I suggest you try to drop the issue and occupy your mind with something more positive.

Am I afraid of being manipulated?

● Nobody can have power over you unless you allow them to. When you do, it's usually because you are subconsciously hoping to gain something. Perhaps a trusted friend could help you to identify what this is.

Do I have difficulties with an overly possessive mother?

● This is one of those problems that are almost impossible to resolve by yourself, so I urge you to seek the help of a therapist. Releasing yourself from your mother's grip could transform your life.

A spider's web is a metaphor for fate. Do you feel uable to change your destiny?

Eating and drinking

Your body needs good food in order to function properly. Yet emotional and spiritual nourishment are also essential for maintaining health and promoting healing.

Dreams about eating and drinking say something about how well you are satisfying your needs in this respect. If you are eating a specific type of food, the dream is encouraging you to assimilate the qualities it represents. The dream could also indicate a need to absorb new attitudes or ideas, or enrich your life with 'soul food'.

Food that's hard to digest represents something you are finding hard to stomach, whilst a dream about refusing to eat implies that you have a poor relationship with your body's needs. Gobbling food or gulping a drink may simply imply greed, but can also suggest a need to cultivate patience and discrimination.

This section focuses on some common dreams featuring food and drink.

Alcohol

Possible meanings

Symbolically speaking, drinking alcohol in a dream often suggests a thirst for spiritual experience. However your dream could also imply that, deep down, you long to feel more relaxed or would like to enjoy a more spirited attitude.

A dream about being drunk has several possible meanings. Perhaps you are intoxicated with someone or something in waking life and need to think more soberly. Maybe you need to lose some of your inhibitions so that you are more receptive to outside influences. If you are a recovering alcoholic though your dream is more likely to be a warning that you are in danger of succumbing to your addictive tendencies.

Questions to ask yourself – and what to do when the answer is 'yes'

Do I yearn for spiritual experience?

● All spiritual traditions emphasize the discipline of daily practice, together with a willingness to serve others. Bearing this in mind, it would now be good to take stock of your life. Where do your priorities lie? What are the values that underpin your actions and your choices? Do you make time for prayer or meditation?

Am I on a high in some area of my waking life?

● You can achieve a great deal when life is so exhilarating. Yet unless you keep your wits about you, you risk losing touch with reality. You may find it useful to talk to someone, perhaps a friend, who has a more objective viewpoint and can help you to keep your feet on the ground.

Am I a recovering alcoholic?

● Please attend your next AA meeting as soon as possible. Your dream implies that you urgently need support.

Alcohol in a dream may show a subconscious desire to let go of your inhibitions.

Starvation

Possible meanings

If you are reading this book, you can probably afford to eat. However, your dream may be a message that you desperately need food for your soul. More rarely, dreaming about starvation can suggest you are so focused on your spiritual or intellectual aspirations that you are neglecting your body's needs.

In view of the intense cultural pressure to be thin, a dream in which you are starving can also reflect a determination to cultivate what you think is an acceptably thin body image.

Since your earliest experience of food was associated with your mother, your dream could indicate that she was unable to provide the emotional sustenance you needed. As a result you may have developed an eating disorder or found it difficult to sustain relationships.

Questions to ask yourself – and what to do when the answer is 'yes'

Do you need to take note of your need for emotional or spiritual nourishment?

Do I need to find a source of soul food?
● Your dream is urging you to make time for pursuits that nurture your inner life. Music, art, gardening or travel are just a few of the many ways of satisfying the needs of your soul. If you tend to live at a frenetic pace, you would find it beneficial to slow down and allow yourself to respond more deeply to your experiences.

Am I ignoring my physical needs in an attempt to be more spiritual?
● The body is the 'temple of the soul' and it deserves your respect. This means supplying it with what it needs to function properly.

Am I obsessed with being thin?
● How will you know when you are thin enough? You are sliding down a slippery slope. It's essential that you learn to value yourself as a real person, not an idealized image. You may need counselling to prevent your obsession from becoming an illness.

Do I feel that my mother failed to meet my emotional needs?
● It's time to heal long-standing emotional wounds. The first step is to understand that holding on to emotions like resentment and bitterness is psychologically harmful and can lead to physical illness. Whatever your mother's shortcomings, you now have to forgive past wrongs and take responsibility for yourself. You may need help from a healer or therapist.

Meat

Possible meanings

Meat was traditionally considered the appropriate food for heroes. Your dream may therefore be encouraging you to cultivate heroic qualities like courage, decisiveness or the ability to focus on a goal and do whatever it takes to achieve it.

A dream about eating meat can also indicate a desire for more sensual satisfaction. Devouring enormous amounts of meat though can mean that you are indulging your animal appetites at the expense of your emotional and spiritual needs.

Alternatively, you may be longing to get your teeth into something meaty, or to find a meatier role in life.

Questions to ask yourself –
and what to do when the answer is 'yes'

Do I need to pursue my goals more vigorously?
● If you are feeling fearful or indecisive, you could find it helpful to imagine that you have reached the end of your life. What do you hope to have achieved by then? From that vantage point, look back at your current situation and offer yourself some advice as to the best way forward.

Am I overriding my sensual needs – or overindulging them?
● It would be good to try and understand what is stopping you from satisfying your basic needs or, at the opposite end of the scale, what is driving you to excess. Do you need to acknowledge a fear that is suppressed, hidden anger or an underlying sense of insecurity that is holding you back?

Would I like to get my teeth into something substantial?
● You could begin by exploring ways of acquiring new skills or polishing up those you already have. It would also be helpful to sort out your priorities so that you don't waste time and energy on trivial issues. If you want more responsibility at work, it would be good to present your boss with some suggestions about how you could expand your role.

Eating meat may reflect a need to absorb the 'meat' or essence of an experience.

Fruit

Possible meanings

If you are fulfilling an ambition or enjoying greater prosperity, your dream reflects the fact that you are in a fruitful phase of your life. It could also mean that a project or a relationship you have been nurturing is now bearing fruit.

Since fruit is associated with fertility, it can feature in your dreams if you are pregnant or trying to conceive.

Eating fruit may also imply enjoying the fruits of your labour. However, a dream about eating soft, sweet luscious fruits like figs and peaches often signifies erotic experiences. Apples, especially, are a traditional symbol of sensual delights and the pleasures of sexuality.

Apples are also associated with Eve's temptation in the Garden of Eden and can therefore represent a tempting opportunity or a tantalizing choice in your life.

Pears can appear in a dream to indicate that an aspect of your life is going 'pear-shaped'.

Questions to ask yourself – and what to do when the answer is 'yes'

Am I hoping to fulfil an ambition?
● The dream is reassuring you that you have done all that is necessary. Soon, you will be in a position to reap the rewards for all the effort and energy you have expended.

Am I pregnant?
● Your dream simply reflects your feelings of well-being now that you are fulfilling your maternal instincts.

Am I in an intensely sexual relationship?
● The dream is a reminder to you that, whilst it's wonderful to luxuriate in sensuality, intimate relationships also need a solid basis of friendship if they are to endure.

Has someone made me a tempting offer?
● Your dream is asking you to be aware of the consequences of choosing to accept the offer. If you know something is wrong but you decide to do it anyway, it may be that subconsciously you have succumbed to temptation in order to teach yourself a valuable lesson.

**Are you currently
enjoying the fruits
of your past efforts?**

Vegetables

Possible meanings

Symbolically speaking, vegetables are associated with spiritual as opposed to sensual or emotional nourishment. Since eating signifies assimilating something, a dream in which you refuse to eat vegetables can indicate that you are neglecting your need for spiritual nourishment.

Vegetables take nutrients from the earth so they sometimes signify your ability to extract something positive from a situation.

A dream about root vegetables can indicate a need to be more grounded or to get in touch with your inner depths. If potatoes feature in your dream, it may be that you are being a 'couch potato'. This sort of tendency is ultimately harmful to your body and your spirit, so your dream is encouraging you to overcome your slothful tendencies and take a more active interest in life.

Questions to ask yourself – and what to do when the answer is 'yes'

Vegetables can signify the spiritual benefits of a particular situation.

Do I need more spiritual nourishment?

● If conventional religion does not meet your needs, you may find that meditation is more satisfying. Depending on your temperament, you could also find spiritual fulfilment through cultivating an appreciation of the arts, exploring your creative potential, or offering your services to a voluntary organization. Taking even a small step towards feeding your spiritual side will help you to start moving in a new direction.

Do I need to see the positive side of a situation?

● When a situation seems hopeless, it can be hard to accept that it may have potential benefits, especially if you are by nature inclined to be pessimistic. Yet if you're willing to try and see the cup as half-full rather than half-empty, a whole new world could open up for you.

Am I out of touch with my innermost thoughts and feelings?

● You probably need to try to lower the volume of your internal 'mind chatter' as you go about your ordinary, everyday activities. Then you will be able to hear the still, small voice within and let it guide you.

Sweets and chocolates

Possible meanings

Sweets and chocolates often symbolize temptations you find too sweet to resist, even though they may not be doing you any good. A dream in which you are gorging yourself with sweets can therefore be warning you against a tendency to self-indulgence.

Your dream could also mean that you want more of the sweet things of life, especially sensual pleasures. Or perhaps you simply feel you deserve a treat!

If you tend to be aggressive, the dream is encouraging you to show the sweeter side of your nature.

Questions to ask yourself –
and what to do when the answer is 'yes'

Am I being self-indulgent?
● It's possible that you are simply being greedy, and need to develop your willpower. Self-indulgence, though, is often a sign of boredom. Your dream may therefore be urging you to find a stimulating challenge. Overindulgence can also be a reaction to feeling that you have been deprived in some area of your life. If so, it would be beneficial to find a more creative way of satisfying those needs.

Do I want more sweetness in my life?
● Perhaps you need to fill your home with flowers, give a party or arrange a weekend away. If sex has become dull or mechanical, it would be good to explore some ways of making it more exciting. If you enjoy art or music, visiting a gallery or going to a concert could make life more agreeable.

Do I need to cultivate my sweeter side?
● There is an old saying that you can achieve far more with honey than with vinegar. Your dream is encouraging you to exercise a little charm. If you feel aggressive because you are stressed, you could benefit from taking more exercise or making time for a calming activity like meditation or yoga.

Sweets in a dream represent tempting sensual pleasures.

Colours

We remember some dreams in black and white whilst others are very definitely in glorious technicolour. Each colour has a traditional symbolic significance, but in your dream it could have a very different meaning, based on a past experience or your current circumstances.

Blue, for instance, is traditionally the colour of spirituality. Yet a dream featuring your friend's glamorous blue designer frock is unlikely to have deep spiritual significance! It's more likely to mean that you envy her sense of style. Always ask yourself then what you associate with the colour in the dream before you apply a more generalized meaning. Remember too that you need to take into account not just the colour of something, but also the object itself.

Red

Possible meanings

The colour red symbolizes sensuality, vitality and intensity. It also implies stimulating activity, excitement and the possibility of danger. We describe someone who has a strong sexual drive as 'red-blooded', whilst the area of town where sex is on offer is known as the 'red-light district'. Red can also represent passionate emotions like rage. 'Seeing red', for instance, implies being very angry.

Questions to ask yourself –
and what to do when the answer is 'yes'

Do I need to express more of my sensuality?

● It may be that you don't really feel comfortable in your body. If you tend to be awkward or clumsy you could consider signing up for dance or drama classes, where you would learn to move with confidence. It may also be time to overhaul your wardrobe and get rid of those shapeless garments that do nothing for you. If you're not sure what suits you, why not enlist the help of an image consultant?

Is there a lack of stimulus in my life?

● If your usual routine has become boring, you would benefit from seeking fresh challenges. What kind of stimulus do you need? Learning a new skill would stretch your intellect. Taking up a sport could galvanize your energy. Or maybe you need to enlarge your circle of friends or involve yourself more closely with your local community.

Am I harbouring feelings of rage?

● Unexpressed anger can sap your vitality, so it's important to find a way of expressing your feelings as soon as possible. If you're afraid of the consequences of showing your anger, please don't hesitate to seek counselling. Rage that's left to smoulder will inevitably explode, possibly in a situation where such a strong reaction is totally unwarranted.

Does the red object remind me of a specific person, situation or period in my life?

● Your dream suggests you have outstanding emotional business relating to whatever this object signifies for you. Your past experience is influencing your reactions to a current situation in a way that's inappropriate. Try to put the past behind you so you can bring a more open mind to what's here and now.

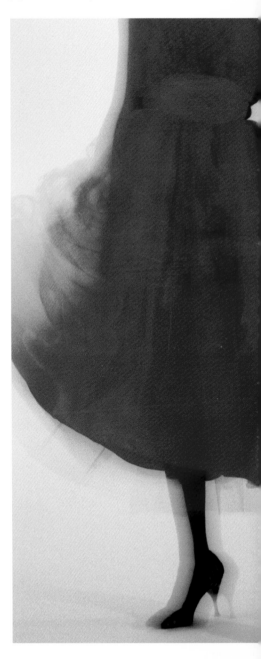

Red is the most stimulating colour, and can signify joyous sensuality.

Blue

Possible meanings

Blue is traditionally the colour of relaxation, tranquillity and healing. It is also associated with spirituality, ideals and intellectual matters. Sometimes, blue implies loyalty and integrity, as in 'true blue'.

The shade of blue in your dream could offer a further clue to its meaning. A dark, mournful shade suggests depression, sadness or disappointment. Light blue can signify intuition, whilst sky blue tends to represent consciousness.

Blue clothes sometimes symbolize masculinity. If you are a woman, your dream could therefore be a message that you need to approach a situation in a more focused or assertive way.

Your dream could also reflect something that has happened 'out of the blue'.

Questions to ask yourself –
and what to do when the answer is 'yes'

Do I need to focus more on my spiritual life?
● Your dream is encouraging you to explore the meaning of your life. You could start by reflecting on your highest values and noticing whether you are actually incorporating them into your daily routine. True spirituality reveals itself in the way you deal with others or cope with difficult circumstances.

Am I feeling blue?
● If you're sitting on your own holding a gloomy conversation with yourself, I recommend that you make an effort to pick up the telephone and talk to a friend or a member of your family. It would also be good to get out of the house and go for a long walk, or to the gym. Physical exercise increases the activity of natural substances in the brain that help to lift your spirits.

Do I need to listen to my intuition?
● First you need to recognize how your intuition manifests itself. Some people can sense a still, small voice within. For others it's a physical sense of unease. Instead of merely dismissing these symptoms as irrational, be open to the possibility that a deeper, wiser part of yourself is trying to tell you something.

Blue is the colour of spirituality in many different cultures.

Green

Possible meanings

When the colour green features in your dream, the meaning varies according to the particular shade. Clear, vibrant green signifies a renewed sense of vitality, potential growth in some area of your life or new developments within your personality. Warm, bright green is associated with healing and creativity. A green light could be a signal to go ahead and do something you've been unsure about in waking life.

Pale green can depict youthful energy or a situation that has yet to develop properly and requires some patience. Dark, muddy shades of green often represent envy or jealousy.

Questions to ask yourself – and what to do when the answer is 'yes'

Am I feeling hopeful about new developments?

● Your dream confirms that your optimism is well-founded. You need not hesitate to embrace the process of change.

Am I recovering from an illness?

● You can rest assured that you are well on the way to renewed health and vigour.

Would I like to explore my creativity?

● Your dream is giving you the go-ahead to start turning your dreams into reality. You may simply need to invest more energy into a current project. Otherwise, it would be good to take a class that will equip you with the basic skills you need.

Am I feeling envious?

● When you envy someone, it means they have something you want. If this relates to a personality trait, your dream is a message that you too can have it. But getting it will mean working at cultivating something that seems to come naturally to the person you envy. Jealousy is more powerful though and can be a much harder emotion to come to terms with. Sometimes only time will heal its corrosive effects. However, you can lessen the impact of your jealous feelings by focusing more on your own well-being. You could benefit from a make-over, learning a new skill, changing your job or even a course of counselling.

Green is associated with fertility and the healing power of nature.

White

Possible meanings

White traditionally symbolizes innocence and purity, which is why it is the colour most often used for wedding dresses. In dreams white can therefore suggest a need to purify yourself of toxic emotions or bad memories. It could also imply a general lack of enthusiasm for life.

A dazzling white light represents mystical experience or spiritual attainment. Yet a dream like this is not necessarily the result of years of spiritual practice. It often comes quite unexpectedly, as if by grace.

If your dream is set in a hospital, white is more likely to mean sickness. The dream may reflect a current health problem, either your own or that of someone close to you. It could also, though, say something about an aspect of your life that needs healing.

Questions to ask yourself – and what to do when the answer is 'yes'

Do I need to cleanse myself of a toxic emotion?
● Negative feelings and experiences are an integral part of being human and can often teach us a valuable lesson. Dwelling on them, though, will only increase their hold over you, so it would be good to starve them of attention. If you are finding it impossible to come to terms with a bad experience, a short course of cognitive therapy would be beneficial.

Am I feeling low?
● If you are in a stressful situation and struggling to cope, you need to ask for help, whether from family members, friends or a professional source. Your spirits should lift once you start feeling less burdened.

Does an area of my life need healing?
● It may be that you're having problems in a relationship and need to meet somebody halfway. If your job is causing problems, the dream could be a message about the need to consider other options.

White can signify the pure, clear awareness of truth.